D1624224

DIARY OF A DREAM

My Journey in
Thoroughbred Racing

by George Rowand

ECLIPSE PRESS

Lexington, Kentucky

Library of Congress Control Number: 2005920846

ISBN-10: 1-58150-127-7
ISBN-13: 978-1-58150-127-8

Printed in the United States of America
First Edition: 2005

Distributed to the trade by
National Book Network
4720-A Boston Way, Lanham, MD 20706
1.800.462.6420

A Division of
Blood-Horse Publications
Publishers Since 1916

*To my wife, Rita, who, when I was failing
badly in the horse business, never once said,
"I think you need to get a real job."*

"Because it's there."

British climber George Mallory when asked why climb Mt. Everest

Standing in the aisle behind the box seats at Hollywood Park on the first Sunday in June in 1991, I was trying to shake off my nervousness. I had made my way from the paddock with my sister and our trainer, and all of us were focused intently on a five-year-old mare named Miss Josh that we were running in the grade I Gamely Handicap. Parading before the stands, she was nibbling on the mane of her lead pony — a good sign. She was eager.

Our seats were upstairs, in the Director's Room, where we had seen some of the owners of the other horses in the field. Hockey great Wayne Gretzky was there, as was a very pregnant Maria Shriver Schwarzenegger. Gretzky had a horse in the field. Famed jockey Bill Shoemaker was there, training the favorite, Fire the Groom, for R.D. Hubbard, the owner of the racetrack. Hubbard had been extremely gracious before the race, coming by our table to make sure everything was all right.

This race was important to us because we were trying to win a championship with Miss Josh, and we needed to win the Gamely, or some other grade I stakes, to have a shot at it. Now, standing there and shifting from foot to foot with about five minutes to go, I was feeling the pressure of a big race.

Our trainer, Barclay Tagg, wasn't sure we should be there. When he had looked at the other fillies and mares in the Gamely, he had seen — on paper at least — that we didn't quite match up in his opinion. He had groused that we might have been better off staying on the East Coast, where we could run shorter distances against horses we knew. I listened politely to what he said and, for once, didn't argue. But I dismissed his complaints as big race nerves. I had seen this side of Barclay long before he won the Kentucky Derby and Preakness with Funny Cide in 2003 and admitted to the world that he was a pessimist by nature. Barclay had been training for us for six years, and while we had already enjoyed success in stakes races together, Barclay knew firsthand how hard the game was, how quickly good fortune could go bad. Even when he was training good horses, apprehension always lurked nearby.

Barclay's face had been tautly drawn when he had saddled Miss Josh in the paddock earlier. My sister and partner, Bonner Young, was really nervous, but that wasn't anything new. Wringing her hands, she kept saying, "I'm so nervous I don't know what to do. I'm so nervous I don't know what to do," but she was always nervous whenever one of our horses ran, whether the purse was high or low, the race important or insignificant. She was an equal-opportunity nervous wreck before a race. She wore a tailored outfit, with a cream-colored jacket and a hat so tall and round that it made me think that she looked like "Hoss" Cartwright's younger, thinner sister, and I started to make a comment to that effect, but I quickly suppressed the idea. Sis was in no mood for levity.

I was dressed in a conservative navy blue suit, white shirt, and dark blue tie with just a touch of pink — one of our racing colors. Eleven years when I quit practicing law, I swore that I would never wear a tie again, but in deference to the significance of the day, I was looking like the lawyer I once had been.

We had Laffit Pincay Jr. in the irons, and that was a very big plus. Laffit was one of the most respected jockeys in the business, a member of racing's Hall of Fame for a decade and a half by then. He had ridden Miss Josh seven months earlier, and she responded with the best race she had ever run. I had great confidence in him.

With only two minutes until post, it was apparent the race wouldn't start on time. The field had not even stepped foot on the turf course, and it would take at least two minutes to load the horses in the gate.

Down in Georgia at a small family gathering, my mother — whose childhood nickname was Miss Josh — was with her sister, Blanche — called Bunky by family and friends. Earlier that day they had attended a service in a tiny church near where they had grown up. Mother confessed that she and Bunky had prayed for Miss Josh. I could just imagine her — three hours and three thousand miles separated from her namesake — checking her watch, subtracting the time difference, and wondering what was going on in California.

I dropped my binoculars case to my feet and kicked it against the railing. When I looked to my right, I saw comedian Tim Conway, dressed in coat and tie, heading for his box seat. I was close enough to hear someone call out to him, "Hey, Tim! Who do you like?" He came right back, "I like Miss Josh. I think she's got a big chance."

"Tim Conway bet on our horse!" I thought.

My mouth was completely dry in anticipation. I hovered somewhere between wanting the race to be over and the outcome known and wanting it never to start. I respected the daunting task I was asking of Miss Josh. Grade I winners come along, roughly speaking, once every thousand foals, and in eighteen months no horse had gone from the East Coast to the West Coast to win a grade I stakes race, so no matter how confident I appeared, deep down I knew it wouldn't be easy. Miss Josh had to fly across the country and cope with a complete change in routine to run on a strange racecourse while the other horses in the field had only to walk out of their stalls and over to the racetrack. That's what's known as a "home field advantage."

I watched through my binoculars as the gate crew began to load the horses two at a time. Miss Josh was one of the last to go in. She stood quietly, and as I watched her, I mumbled to myself a nonsense phrase, as I always did before a start.

"Come on, Laffit! Get her out and get her up! Come on, Laffit! Bring her home!"

Laffit pulled his goggles over his eyes and leaned forward. Miss Josh was standing well, her eyes looking straight through the slots at the turf course that stretched away from her.

The bell sounded, and the field bounded away, with Miss Josh making a good clean start. Laffit folded into a crouch and began to look for a way to ease Miss Josh toward the rail to save some ground before they got to the first turn. Up in his booth overlooking the track, race announcer Trevor Denman called out, in his clipped South African accent, "Miss Josh, in the pink, is tugging away at the bit in fourth."

It had taken a long time for me to get to this day, eighteen years in fact. I was a college kid when I first heard the call, the siren song of horse racing. I had never grown up around horses, never owned a horse, never knew anyone who owned horses. To conceive of the dream, as I did, of not only owning racehorses — the top of the pyramid when it comes to horses — but owning champion racehorses was truly ludicrous. Yet I was driven to make it happen, "Dedicated to breeding and racing the Champion," as the motto on our stationery said.

Now in front of me, played out on a grassy green stage, was the possible culmination of that dream. Miss Josh was sitting comfortably in fourth, waiting for Pincay to ask her for her best. As they spun around the first turn and headed down the backstretch, Laffit sat stone still. I didn't know it until later, but I was watching the most professional piece of race-riding any of our horses ever received.

I peeked quickly at the timer on the toteboard and saw, to my satisfaction, that the early fractions were not too fast. Good. Miss Josh had plenty of early speed — too much for her own good on occasion — but Laffit had gotten her to relax behind a reasonable pace, and when I looked again and saw that the first half-mile had been run in :48 1/5, with Miss Josh sitting three lengths back, I knew we were live. She had gotten the pace scenario she needed to run her best race. Now she faced the most important question: Was she good enough?

As I watched the race through my high-powered binoculars, I could hear the voices in the crowd — especially our group — begin to rise, urging on their horses. With a half-mile to run, Laffit let out the reins just a touch on Miss Josh. She began to cut into the lead of the three horses ahead of her, but it was a subtle move, inch by inch. Only the second time aboard her, Pincay had figured out this mare.

As they turned for home, Laffit got to the leader. To the left of me, I could hear somebody yell, "Come on, Gary! Get her going!" My brain told me that the person was yelling for Gary Stevens, aboard the favorite, the stretch-running Fire the Groom. Above the din nearby, I could hear Trevor Denman call, "Fire the Groom has ten to make up," yet when I looked back, it was more like three or four, but I could see that Stevens had extricated his horse from some traffic and at last she was moving.

Up ahead, with just an eighth of a mile to go, Laffit had taken the lead with Miss Josh, and it was there, with about two hundred yards to run that he turned up his stick, popped her twice right-handed, and asked her for what she had. She surged but didn't pull away from Island Jamboree to her outside, while on the inside Fire the Groom kept closing the margin.

By then I was yelling so vigorously that from the quarter pole to the wire my voice went from normal to hoarse. Miss Josh had the lead, Laffit was riding vigorously, and they were rapidly approaching the wire. With one hundred yards to go, I realized that she couldn't be beaten. She was holding Island Jamboree safe, and Fire the Groom's final charge was faltering. It was fifty yards and Miss Josh still had the lead, then forty, thirty, twenty, and ten yards. Island Jamboree was trying hard, Fire the Groom was giving her all, and Miss Josh, our girl, the one whose mating we had planned, whose birth we had eagerly awaited, and whose career had been so iffy because of her lousy feet, put her nose on the wire.

Everything good in life, it seems to me, begins with a dream, and how I got to that place and time is the story I want to tell. While many subjects in life may be debatable, a story about the realization of a person's dream is a different matter. Anybody who has begun the quest to achieve a dream probably can tell you down to the second where it was that the passion of his life grabbed him. I know I can. Years after the fact, when people asked me how I got into the horse business, the answer was always the same:

"I saw Secretariat."

I saw Secretariat run — really run — for about fifteen seconds, and my life was never the same. Neither were the lives of those close to me. Even now, it's difficult to believe that so much could have been riding on that one tiny slice of my existence.

Chapter 2

I entered law school in Memphis in 1971, and whenever I was home for a break, I would go to the track, either Charles Town or the Maryland tracks, often with my best friend, Joe Illig, whom I had known since junior high. Like most newcomers to racing, we struggled at the betting windows. That lack of success drove me to learn something about the art of picking a winner, and gradually my winning increased.

In the fall of 1972, at a time when Secretariat dominated the sports pages, I decided to take the *Daily Racing Form* for a month as a diversion from school. While perusing the pages, I saw a tiny ad for tickets to the Preakness Stakes the following May, and I ordered two, one for myself and one for Joe. I decided I had to see this phenom with my own eyes. Winner of eight of his nine starts at two, (though disqualified from one victory), he was said to be strong, talented, and charismatic. One other thing intrigued me about the horse. He was a Virginian, and I knew the area where he had been foaled and raised.

I followed Secretariat during the spring of 1973, by then convinced that he was a great horse. It had been twenty-five years since a horse had won the Triple Crown, the toughest test in American racing, and it seemed to me that Secretariat had what it took to conquer the triumvirate.

Secretariat started off the year winning impressively. He took the Bay Shore Stakes at seven-eighths of a mile and then ran even better in the one-mile Gotham. His next start, just two weeks before the Kentucky Derby, was the Wood Memorial, at a mile and one-eighth. There he failed, finishing a struggling third behind Angle Light and Sham, the big chestnut's main Derby threat.

People started jumping to conclusions: he wasn't sound, he was sick, and — most cutting of all — he was genetically unable to run a classic distance.

On Derby Day, I was at the Virginia Gold Cup, the biggest steeplechase race in Virginia. Illegal bookies offered 3-2 odds on Secretariat and his entry mate, Angle Light, and I bet ten dollars on the duo. Someone had a television in the field, and people packed around it to watch the Derby after the Virginia races were over. I crouched behind the TV, near the speaker, and listened to Chic Anderson call the race for CBS.

When the race started, a sprinter named Shecky Greene broke on top, took the lead, and scooted away. Sham, under jockey Laffit Pincay, was in a perfect spot, close to the rail and close to the lead. Secretariat broke last and stayed dead last the first quarter-mile.

I strained to hear Anderson call Secretariat's name, but being so far back early, the big chestnut didn't even get a mention for the first quarter-mile or so. Then, under the able hands of Ron Turcotte, he started making up ground, and all at once, Anderson said that Secretariat was sixth and moving. On the turn for home, Pincay sent Sham after Shecky Greene. They tussled for the lead a bit, but Laffit was on a horse with gas in his tank while the sprinter was running on fumes. Sham took the lead, with Secretariat sweeping into third. Secretariat rolled to Sham, ran with him a sixteenth of a mile or so, and then went past him, winning easily and breaking the track record.

I leapt to my feet, slapped hands with people nearby, and went off to collect my race winnings. I watched the race over and over that night on the news and read everything I could find about the horse. It turned out that when racing pundits analyzed the way Secretariat ran the race, they discovered that he ran each quarter-mile faster than the preceding quarter, an incredible achievement for any running athlete.

Two weeks later Joe and I were off to Pimlico, site of the Preakness, where it turned out we had terrible seats. They were low and on the first turn, so when horses were running along the backstretch, we couldn't see them over the toteboard in the infield, and when they turned for home, they were running straight at us. Our only good view was that of the first turn, but as fate would have it, that vantage point was just right to watch Secretariat make his move.

The Preakness had just six horses, only three of which stood a legitimate chance — Secretariat, Sham, and Our Native, who had run a distant third in the Kentucky Derby.

A little past 5:30 p.m. on May 19, the starter set the sextuplet free from the gate. Secretariat broke slowly and was last as the field sprinted toward the first turn. Joe and I stood on our chairs as the horses approached, and I could see the field clearly. As Secretariat neared us, his jockey, Ron Turcotte, eased him outside the pack. Boom! The big colt exploded, leaping into gear and taking off after the leaders. All at once it seemed like the other horses were doing forty miles an hour and he was doing sixty. His move was absolutely electrifying. The crowd roared in appreciation. They had come to see something special, and here it was, right in front of them.

"He moved too soon," Joe called out above the clamor.

"No, he's okay," I shouted. But what did I know? I was guessing and hoping at the same time.

When they went out of sight, we strained to listen to the call of the announcer as the noise of the record crowd rose to a frenzy at the unfolding scene.

Laffit Pincay sent Sham up after the big red horse, tracking him into the turn. Upstairs, Chic Anderson called out, "They're on the turn, and here's the race, folks."

Joe and I craned to see the stretch run. I could see the big red colt with the blue-and-white blocks on his blinkers' hood in the lead. I could see that Sham was not threatening, and Anderson called out, "But Turcotte has his whip put away, and Secretariat has them put away! He's beginning to draw away!" Then it was over. Secretariat had won again, by the same two and a half-lengths margin as the Derby.

I got down off that chair, giddy with excitement from the brilliant performance I had just witnessed. After we watched Secretariat gallop past us toward the winner's circle, I turned to Joe and said, "I'd like to have a horse like that some day."

Three weeks later Secretariat went into the Belmont Stakes a recognized star. Appearing on the covers of *Time*, *Newsweek*, and *Sports Illustrated*, Secretariat transcended the sport. Even people who knew nothing about racing were swept up in the hoopla of his quest for what only a month earlier had been considered almost impossible. He was going for the elusive Triple Crown, and everybody wanted to watch.

His toughest foe appeared to be his old competitor, Sham. There were a couple of new horses, but they posed little threat, considering that Secretariat had won the Preakness almost eased up. If he ran his race he should win, and everybody knew it.

I watched the race on TV, as nervous as if I owned him. On the biggest stage of his career, Secretariat didn't just run his race. He ran the race of his life. He took the lead coming out of the gate and raced Sham into submission.

Announcer Chic Anderson found it difficult to describe what he was witnessing: "Secretariat is moving like a tremendous machine!" Anderson called out as the horse neared the finish line. "Secretariat by twelve ... Secretariat by fourteen! ... Secretariat by twenty-two lengths! He is going to be the Triple Crown winner!" Anderson called with the big horse 110 yards from the wire.

And then it was over. Secretariat won the classic race by an incredible thirty-one lengths, setting a world record for the distance on dirt, winning the Triple Crown, and cementing a dream in my heart.

With Secretariat as the inspiration, I was absolutely certain that I had to find a way to get into the game. Looking at my prospects objectively, I knew the odds were against me owning a stable of racehorses. I had a career as a small-town attorney staring at me, and while attorneys like that might make a decent living, they generally didn't earn enough to indulge in a passion for fast horses.

Yet, like anybody who dreams about doing anything, I never considered the odds against succeeding. I was sure that I was going to own race-horses one day, and that's all there was to it.

When I went back to law school in the fall of 1973, instead of concentrating full time on my law courses, I read about great horse breeders, famous jockeys and trainers, and stories of horses that came from humble beginnings to become stars.

I finished law school in May 1974, and on my way home to Virginia from Memphis, my father and I detoured through Kentucky. I had written to Seth Hancock, the president of Claiborne Farm, to ask if we could see Secretariat, and he had quickly replied and invited us to come by. Secretariat was in his paddock when we arrived, and the groom took us down the lane to the magnificent chestnut's fence. He came rushing over to see who we were, and when he stuck his nose over the fence two feet from me, his presence took my breath away. He was as handsome and as charismatic up close as I thought he'd be. I couldn't have been more excited if I had met royalty or a movie star.

I continued studying all aspects of racing. It is a family trait that whenever something strikes our interest, we try to find out everything we can about the subject. My father was like that, and looking back on things now, I can see he passed it on to me. I read everything I could find about racing and breeding. I took books out of the library and subscribed to *The Blood-Horse* magazine and *The Thoroughbred Record*. I read the *Daily Racing Form* and started corresponding with some of the writers, first with Abram Hewitt, the Virginia columnist, and then with Leon Rasmussen, the breeding columnist. Rasmussen recommended that I read books by Franco Varola, an Italian lawyer who had some interesting theories about breeding horses. I did, and I read others as well, including one written by Federico Tesio, probably the greatest private breeder of the twentieth century. Really, if a book was about racehorses, I'd read it.

In pursuit of my horse dreams, I took advantage of what was available to me, living in Manassas at the time, so close to the horse country of northern Virginia. Every spring Trinity Episcopal Church in Upperville presented a fund-raiser called the Stable Tour, during which local residents would open their farms to visitors. One of the farms was Paul Mellon's famous Rokeby. Mellon, owner and breeder of the 1971 English Derby winner Mill Reef, had a beautiful, immaculate place. Walking through the barn was like walking through racing's Hall of Fame. Almost every mare had produced a famous horse or was famous in her own right, or both. I remember the awe I felt when I went into the stable and saw Fort Marcy, Horse of the Year in 1970, just standing in a stall. The 1976 tour included a yearling from the first crop of Secretariat. I rushed to the stall to see a smallish, chestnut colt that was a half brother to Arts and Letters, the winner of the 1969 Belmont Stakes. (Later named Debrett, the colt was nothing special as a racehorse. Goes to show you good parents often don't mean much in racing.)

As for a legal career that would be successful enough to enable me to buy racehorses, it wasn't to be. Quite simply, I wasn't interested in practicing law. I hated sitting in an office all day, and I cared neither for the combative nature of the courtroom nor for the dullness of the work in general. What kept me going was my fantasy life, in which I already was a horse owner. When I went to the track — which I did every weekend — I would go to the paddock, look at the people, and wonder, "What must it feel like to have a horse in a race?"

The first horse sale my sister and I went to was a small-time affair held in a tent in Warrenton, Virginia, where the top price was $7,500. The following spring we went to Timonium, Maryland, to a sale of two-year-olds. When the first horse through the ring brought five thousand dollars, my sister and I turned to each other in amazement. We couldn't believe that someone would spend that much money, just like that. But then other horses followed, and the prices were even higher. I wondered if I could ever find a way to get the excess cash to get into the horse business even with my sister as a partner. My sister Bonner, six years older than I, hadn't shown any interest in racing until I got the bit in my teeth. An animal lover at heart, she enjoyed being around the horses, especially the young ones.

In 1977 the two of us went to "A Day in Kentucky," a program sponsored by the Kentucky Thoroughbred Breeders. We arrived in Lexington a day early so we could visit several stud farms and see the stallions. We were like two kids in a candy shop. We went to Claiborne, Greentree, Spendthrift, Gainesway, and a couple of other farms. Late in the day we arrived at Darby Dan Farm, where we met famed Kentucky horseman Olin Gentry, the farm manager. I had always liked Darby Dan horses, and I started talking to Gentry about the Darby Dan horses that I had seen run — Roberto, Little Current, and a favorite, True Knight. I told him that we had come to see the stallions, and Gentry sat at the typewriter and slowly typed out a note to give to a stallion groom. It said, "Please take this gentleman down the lane to see the stallions. He is a horseman." Gentry was the first person ever to call me a horseman, and — even though it wasn't true — I kept the note. I still have it in my scrapbook.

At the program, we met a woman from Cot Campbell's Dogwood Stable, who later took down our names and phone numbers. Cot was one of the first people to make a business of syndicating racehorses, which is a simple idea, really. Basically the horse is split into shares, and the shares are sold. Costs and income are split among the shareholders. It is a good way to limit the risk of ownership.

A couple of weeks later I came back into the office from court one day to find that Cot Campbell had called. My heart jumped!

"Cot Campbell called me?" I asked the secretary, incredulously. "That man buys millions of dollars of horses every year. Why would he call me?"

I flew upstairs to my office, taking the steps two at a time, and called Cot. He was as gracious as a Georgian should be, saying he was just following up on the lead from the Kentucky program. He wanted to see if I might be interested in buying a piece of a racehorse. I hemmed and hawed, and then he said that he had a couple of shares left in an inexpensive filly. Could he send me some information?

"Why not," I said.

A couple of days later I received a photo of the filly, the pedigree information, and the costs associated with a share in her. It was way too much for me, and I called him back to tell him. He was kind and promised to check in with me periodically to see if I would want to buy a share in other horses. Cot didn't take himself too seriously, and I liked that.

The years ticked away. I saw Affirmed beat Alydar in the Laurel Futurity in 1977 and watched Spectacular Bid — who cost a mere $37,000 as a yearling — dominate that race the following year. I was heartened by the idea that, while horses like Affirmed and Alydar were bred by their owners, every year it seemed that relatively cheap horses were winning important races.

Meanwhile, I practiced law. My boss was the Commonwealth's Attorney, the prosecuting attorney for Prince William County, and I was a civil associate. He later would handle the criminal trials for Lorena Bobbitt and her husband, and in the fall of 2003 he prosecuted one of the suspects in the D.C. sniper case. The profession suited me less and less, but I didn't know what else to do. Then, in late 1979, fate intervened once again. The Virginia General Assembly changed the law that had permitted Commonwealth's Attorneys to have civil practices. Now my choice was clear: I either had to leave the office or become an assistant Commonwealth's Attorney.

I didn't much like the idea of becoming a prosecutor, but I was scared I might not be able to do anything else. I applied for an assistant prosecutor position. My boss said that he would consider my application and let me know. The law went into effect on January 1, 1980, and as we reached the end of December I still didn't know where I stood. Finally, on the morning of Christmas Eve, 1979, I was alone in the office with him. I went in and asked if he had made up his mind. He was very direct.

"I don't think that you're cut out to be an attorney," he said in his opening statement, and I didn't hear whatever else he had to say.

I'm out of a job, I thought. It's Christmas. What am I going to do?

Chapter 3

*T*here's nothing like getting fired on Christmas Eve to get your attention. Yet by making what had been my worst fear into a reality my former boss had done me a favor. He had told me the truth. I was going nowhere as an attorney, and I never would have been better than average. I thought I needed a complete change of careers, and when I saw a newspaper ad for a State Department job, I decided to apply.

"Maybe I'll be able to travel," I told myself.

The application process took months. I went to interview after interview and took tests and physicals, passing one round just to await another. Meanwhile, I finished up what was left of my law practice and continued to go to the racetrack and to study bloodlines.

In April my sister, brother-in-law, and I attended the Arkansas Derby with some friends who lived in Kansas but who spent the Oaklawn racing season at the track in Hot Springs. Leaving the track after Temperence Hill won the Arkansas Derby, I got into the car and — for some reason unknown to me now — I proceeded to recite the prior twenty-five winners of the Kentucky Derby off the top of my head. I think that our Kansas friends, Bill and Bobbie Allam, were impressed, because when we got back to their lake house and sat around relaxing, Bill said, "I tell you what. Tom (Young, my brother-in-law) here will give you $10,000, and I'll give you $10,000, and you go buy a racehorse and manage it for us, and we'll give you a free share."

I thought, "They put up the money, and I get to manage a racehorse, and I get a free share? Where's the downside in this? I'll do it!"

I wasn't sure that Bill was serious, and my hopes were punctured when I got home and told Fred Kohler, a friend from church in Middleburg who owned and bred horses, about the plan.

"It's not enough money," he said.

"He should know," I thought. I put aside the plan and waited for news from the government.

I went to my final interview in June, and it all seemed good. The man interviewing me said he was going to make his decision in the next few days, and everything he said sounded positive. The following Tuesday I received a letter from the State Department. I hadn't been hired.

"Now what will I do?" I asked myself. I had been certain I was going to get that job, but now that I had not, I felt lost. I was thirty-two and without a job or prospects for a job.

My sister Bonner was at the beach at the time, and she knew I had applied for the State Department job. I called her, and she asked what I wanted to do, and I spoke right from the heart.

"I tell you what I'd like to do," I said. "I'd like to get $100,000 together and go buy two yearling fillies and get into the racing business. That's what I'd like to do."

We ended our conversation there. I hung up the phone, and when it rang twenty minutes later, I had a case of precognition. I knew it was going to be my sister, and I knew she was going to say we could do it. I picked up the phone. It was my sister.

"I think we can do this," she was saying, and I was calm as she explained how we could raise $100,000 and whom we could have as partners.

We started calling friends and offering them the chance to buy into our syndicate. We called the Allams first, and they were in, just like they said they would be. My mother was eager to participate and to my surprise, my father agreed to come through with the cash to be a part of the horse syndicate. It surprised me because, first, as conservative as he was financially I couldn't believe he would spring for $10,000. And secondly, his only real experience with horses when he was growing up occurred when one of his brothers ran away from home to join the circus and came home months later with a horse as his pay when the circus went broke.

To my father, a horse represented more work. He liked machinery better.

That was as much commitment as we could get, and it wasn't enough if we were going to raise $100,000.

Tom Young, Bonner's husband, said that he would come through with $70,000, so that gave us $90,000. Close enough. We made plans to go to the Keeneland fall sale to buy two yearling fillies. As we prepared, I assessed my own skill set. I was confident in my ability to analyze pedigrees, yet I knew I was in over my head in understanding conformation. What we needed, I thought, was somebody to check out the physical aspects of the horses and help us place a value on them.

We had heard of a Virginian who was so well known in the horse business that people referred to him by his first name only, like some equine rock star. His name was Tyson, and he lived about an hour from our home.

Educated at Princeton, Tyson Gilpin was what one could call a true Virginia gentleman. Tall, graceful, with a full head of white hair, Tyson was an elegant man who wore black tie to the yearling sales at Saratoga, where he had been a consignor for decades. He was as nimble negotiating a breeding contract to a popular stallion as he was two-stepping around a dance floor. He knew his horses, knew the players in the game, and was a lot of fun to be around. Yet, like a lot of well-bred gentlemen, he had his quirks. For one, he always was buying and driving the rattiest old cars, often with the hubcaps missing.

"Drive them at least 175,000 miles," he advised me. "Two hundred thousand is even better."

When we spoke with him, he said what we wanted to do was fine … that buying fillies was logical because even if they couldn't run, they could be turned into broodmares. Thus, one had two chances to get lucky.

"Who knows, you might buy the next Genuine Risk," he said, referring to the first filly to win the Kentucky Derby in sixty-five years — a feat accomplished that spring.

A few weeks later the Keeneland catalogs came, and I was so excited, you would have thought it was Christmas. I knew plenty of good horses were in the sale, potential stakes winners, maybe even champions. All we had to do was to find them. I stayed up looking at those pedigrees until 4 a.m. and really wasn't tired when I finally turned in. I was so wired! I found a lot of fillies we thought we could afford.

My sister and I decided to name our racing stable Bonner Farm after our grandfather on our mother's side. He was a wonderful man from Georgia who enjoyed sports and good times, and he surely would have relished going to the races with us, we thought.

When we got to the sale, we looked at a lot of fillies and narrowed the field down to one filly to bid on that Sunday, the opening day. I wasn't crazy about her pedigree, but I wasn't sure how to tell Tyson. My sister and I were a little past nervous when we went into the sales arena to bid. Tyson, of course, had done this hundreds of times before, so it was just another day at the office for him.

The bidding opened up and bounced along slowly before Tyson eventually got in with a bid of $25,000. Then we exchanged bids with one other bidder in thousand-dollar increments. When the other person bid $30,000, the auctioneer asked for $32,000. Tyson held up one finger, and they took it at $31,000. The other bidder went to $32,000, and we quit. My sister and I walked out of the arena feeling great. We had been in the game. We had come close. We had gotten nervous. And we had not bought a filly that — we found out later — would fall over dead the next year while training at Newmarket, England.

In addition we were invited as guests with Tyson to a party that night. We had been in the horse business one day and already we were part of the social scene. How could we have had a better start than that?

The next horse we decided to bid on was a filly from the consignment of Hidaway Farm, which is near Paris, Kentucky. She was selling Tuesday afternoon, and we already had her name picked out — Audacity, from a quote from General George Patton: "An army needs three things to succeed in battle: self-confidence, speed, and audacity." When I first read that, it sounded like the prescription for success in racing. A racehorse needed speed to be good, and we hoped she had it. I had the self-confidence of the uninitiated. And the idea of doing what we wanted to do was audacious enough for us.

On Monday afternoon we looked at another filly on our original list. She was in the last crop of Pia Star, an older stallion who had been successful without ever having had a top horse to his credit. The filly was the first foal out of her dam, a mare that had raced well in California in the 1970s. She was in the Taylor Made Farm consignment, and we asked Duncan Taylor about the mare.

"The mare has a Master Derby colt by her side and is in foal to Seattle Slew and is going back to Seattle Slew," the consignor reported.

Those facts moved this filly up our list.

"Look, even if she can't run, it's possible that she could be the half sister to a top horse in a couple of years, and then what would she be worth?" Bonner and I said to each other.

This filly became our number one choice, which was tough since she came up on Wednesday, and we wouldn't know how much we would have left to spend until after Audacity had sold. I checked the sales of yearlings by Pia Star and discovered his babies averaged about $25,000. I thought this filly would bring that much, plus one bid, which could put her at $27,000 or $30,000. Thirty thousand dollars should get her, I thought.

Audacity was led into the ring on Tuesday afternoon, and we started bidding at about $20,000. When we hit $30,000, my heart was pounding. That was as far as we wanted to go, and we hoped that would be enough. After several pleas from the auctioneer, the other bidder went to $32,000. We didn't hesitate. Tyson bid $35,000, and the auctioneer looked to the other bidder. "Will you go $37,000? … $37,000? I'm gonna sell her. Won't you try her one more time?" Meanwhile, I'm dying. "Knock that hammer down!" I thought. The whole sale took less than two minutes, but it surely was the longest two minutes of my life. "Yes or no," the auctioneer was saying to the other bidder. "I'm gonna sell her," he warned one more time. He brought the hammer up and looked right at the other bidder. Bang!

She was ours! I shook hands with Tyson and hugged my sister. The runner brought the receipt for Tyson to sign, and when that was done, we jumped up and went back to the barn to see our first racehorse.

Hidaway Farm owner Tom Hinkle was there with his brother Henry, and he asked a question:

"Was that your last bid? Would you have gone any higher?"

"That was it," I told him. It actually was five thousand dollars more than I had wanted to spend, but who's counting when you're buying racehorses that might become something important?

Audacity shipped to a boarding farm in Virginia the next day. We watched her get on the van and then turned our attention to the Pia Star filly. At breakfast Tyson said we shouldn't go past about $35,000, but with $45,000 still in the bank, I meant to get that filly.

The day dragged on, and eventually hip number 914 was led in. My sister decided to stand out back, behind the arena, while the bidding went on. She wanted to be there when the filly came out of the ring and follow her back to the barn if she was ours.

The bidding started off unremarkably at five thousand dollars. We jumped in at $18,000. Someone else bid $20,000, and we came back at $22,000. I thought we were going to get her right then and there, but a $25,000 bid came from someone else, and I turned to see our agent nod when the auctioneer asked for $27,000. Out back my sister was breathing in short bursts, but inside I actually was pretty calm. I thought the bidding had run its course, and I could see we were the most insistent. The bid spotter asked for $30,000 from the underbidder, and failing to get that, the spotter motioned with his hands that the bidder was done. The hammer came down. We had bought our filly.

I found my sister, and we went to the barn. It was well past mid-afternoon, and the shadows were lengthening. I hoisted myself atop the wall across the shed row from the filly's stall and watched her as she moved around in the stall. This one, more than Audacity, left me with the feeling that, at last, my dream was coming true. I was in the horse business.

Chapter

"They'll never be successful.
You can't learn the horse business from a book."

Words spoken by a Virginia horsewoman we knew
when she heard we were going into the horse business.

Unsolicited opinion aside, we were having fun in the horse business, and we didn't think that the dreadful odds against success could possibly apply to us. We eagerly awaited the opportunity to go to the Middleburg boarding farm Tyson had recommended we use.

The woman running the boarding farm took one look at Audacity and the Pia Star filly — whom we had taken to calling the Other One — and gave us her opinion:

"If I were starting a racing stable, I wouldn't have bought these two," she said. "And I had my brother — who's a trainer — look at them, and he agreed with me."

That attitude bothered us in the beginning, but we ogled every move the fillies made, no matter what. We went to see them every week and decided just to turn them out into a large paddock and let them grow rather than break them that fall.

When we applied for names for the girls, we discovered the name Audacity was already taken. We came back with something similar. In the movie *Patton*, the general was trying to put some starch in a general he had asked to make an assault in Sicily. He had said, "Remember what Frederick the Great said, *L'audace, l'audace, toujours l'audace.*"

I liked that. We applied for and received Toujours L'Audace, and it seemed to suit this daughter of Intrepid Hero. Tyson especially liked it. "Great name," he told me on a number of occasions. "Great name."

For the Other One, we wanted Highland Girl, as my niece was attending a school named Highland, and we wanted to name the filly for her. That name was taken, so we came back with a variation on her dam's name, Le Moulin, which means "the windmill" in French. We named her Highland Mills.

That November my buddy Joe Illig died. He was thirty-two years old, had been married only three years, and had an eight-month-old son.

Joe's death impacted me in a way I hadn't expected. Up until then I had planned on getting another job while running Bonner Farm on the side. Like most people our age, I thought I had all the time in the world. Joe's death brought a different idea home.

The thought came to me that I'd better get going in the horse business, that maybe I didn't have the time I thought I did.

I decided to apply myself full time to Bonner Farm. I was afraid that if I were working someplace else and the horse venture failed, I would forever wonder if it would have succeeded had I applied myself 100 percent.

I wasn't married. Living with my family, I had no mortgage or rent payments. The partners were paying for the upkeep of the horses, and I was drawing a small stipend to keep me going. Plus, I had some extra income from betting. The summer of 1980 I devised my own system of very conservative handicapping. On average, I would bet twice a week, but my system was so solid that I didn't lose a single bet that entire summer. It also taught me something about the successful placement of horses in races.

I went to the library and researched every race that Le Moulin had run. I looked at every chart and discovered she had been effective on the grass at a distance of a mile and a sixteenth. She had beaten some important fillies in California, even though she was not a stakes winner, and she had raced as a homebred for Howard Keck, one of Claiborne Farm's clients. I liked that connection. The further back in the pedigree I looked, the more Claiborne influence I saw. I thought the family might be better than it looked on paper, and with the new owner willing to breed Le Moulin to the likes of Seattle Slew, I thought the female line really had a chance.

That spring I spoke with a bloodstock agent I knew who was a part of a new group that was measuring horses. This group looked at a horse as a biomechanical machine. The idea was to measure the various angles and lengths of bone to determine whether a horse was put together well enough to become a good runner. I was intrigued. I had the two fillies measured, and the reports came back a week or so later.

When they measured Audacity (we still called her that, no matter what The Jockey Club thought), the measurers said she was a quality filly, perhaps a stakes-quality filly, just as we thought. And they thought she would make a good broodmare as well. As for Highland Mills, they weren't so encouraging. Her numbers weren't good, and the author of the report had been succinct: "Unless you're an outright gambler, don't even bother putting her in training. Just get her in-foal and sell her as an unraced three year old."

We didn't listen to that advice. Why should we? Ignoring the advice of "experts" is one of the best things about horse racing. Oil man Bill Allam told me something useful about his business that I carried over to the horse business: "If the geologists were as good as they think they are, they'd have all the oil." If the horse experts were as good as they think they are, they'd have bought Seattle Slew, Spectacular Bid, Genuine Risk, and all the other top runners that sold so cheaply.

We had the two fillies broken in the spring of 1981 and then turned them out for the summer. We said we were trying to give them a chance to grow, but the real reason was we didn't know what to do with them next. Audacity, our big hope, already had experienced some swelling in her ankles, but we were pretty sure it wouldn't prevent her from becoming a good horse.

Meanwhile, I was continuing my education by attending as many horse sales as I could, meeting horsemen, and paying attention to what they said and did. We started assembling the next syndicate group. We still were in the market for fillies because of the "residual value" we thought they had, though when I told a bloodstock agent that idea at the 1981 Keeneland July sale, he scoffed.

After watching females bring outrageous prices and hearing auction-eers stop the proceedings to say about some well-bred filly that "she's worth more than that if she never steps foot on the racetrack," lifelong horseman Russell Jones still wasn't impressed with our strategy.

"How much 'residual value' do you think a filly's going to have if you pay twice what she's worth in the first place?" he snorted.

We raised $80,000, went through the sales catalogs, and went back to Keeneland that fall with Tyson. Prices for fillies were still soaring, and it was difficult to buy, but eventually we found two we thought we could afford and bought the first one through the ring for $47,000. The pedigree wasn't nearly as good as what we had bought just one year earlier. She was by a a very large stallion named Turn and Count and out of a mare named Silent Choice, who I was told later was very small. A bay filly, she had a twinkle in her eye that we liked, but she was tall and didn't seem long enough in the back to me. Yet, I was sent to the sale to buy a filly, not to come home with tales of how hard it was, so we bought a filly. When the other filly went through the ring for $60,000, in our price range, I had an immediate sick feeling in my stomach. We had liked her better but thought we had to bid on the first one if she fell in our price range. I left Keeneland feeling like we had gotten the second-best horse we saw.

When we shipped our new purchase to Virginia, the woman who ran the boarding farm where our other two horses were stabled took one look at her and gave a quick appraisal: "She has no substance." Not knowing what that meant, we didn't have a response.

Looking for a name, we turned to others for suggestions. John Antus, our sister Marj's husband, came up with the winner. He said what we real-ly were pursuing was a "fragile dream," and that's the name The Jockey Club approved.

After returning from the sales, we decided it finally was time to send Audacity and Highland Mills to a training track. We chose Rocketts Mill Farm in Doswell, Virginia, near where Secretariat had grown up. The farm was owned and run by Ed Stevens, a tough, good-hearted individual who was lively and funny. A former college football player, Stevens was one of few who could claim to weigh less as an adult than he did in college.

"I'm one who truly can say that I lost my butt in the horse business," he joked.

Stevens had built a boarding and breaking operation in rural Hanover County, just north of Richmond. His training track was a half-mile oval, and he stood stallions and bred mares as well.

My sister and I went down to Rocketts Mill the day after the fillies shipped the one hundred miles from Middleburg. We were beginning to become accustomed to being greeted with criticism directed at our horses. Stevens took one look at the fillies and wasn't impressed by them or their training to that point. Of course, we knew something that he and the other critics didn't: that Audacity was destined to become a stakes horse; it was just a matter of time.

"They're real giddy-up-and-stop horses," he said.

Ed started them out easily, and they began to muscle up and get fitter. Surprisingly, the riders liked Highland Mills better than Audacity.

Meanwhile, Sis and I went around to other horse farms in Virginia, Maryland, and Kentucky. We were trying to learn as much as we could about the game, and there's nothing like seeing horses close up. Now we had the chance to see Secretariat a couple of times a year. It was always a treat to see that charismatic individual, and one day I decided, "What the heck." I went over and hugged him. Professional horsemen weren't supposed to do that, but what did I care?

In October 1981, we went to Buckland Farm just up the road from us in Gainesville, Virginia. Buckland's homebred colt, Pleasant Colony, had won the Kentucky Derby and Preakness that year on the way to being named champion three-year-old, and he was back on the farm for a little rest and relaxation before going to Kentucky to start his new career as a stallion. We were standing in his paddock as he circled quietly around us. Farm manager Don Robertson talked about him and then did something I hadn't expected. He offered us a share in him.

Here we were, nobodies in the sport, and he was offering us a share in that year's champion. I was stunned. We were moving up, I thought. Foolishly, I turned him down, not because of the share price of $300,000, but rather because I had serious doubts about Pleasant Colony's being a successful stallion.

We watched our own fillies work out at least once a week, but being so new to the process, we couldn't tell much. One day toward the end of 1981, Ed called to say that it was time to send Audacity on … to the breeding shed. Her racing career was over before it had begun.

"Her ankles won't let her go on," he said. "She's through."

We were devastated. The first horse we had bought, the one that was going to be a stakes winner, and she was done before even getting to the racetrack? How could this be?

We asked Tom Hinkle if we could board her at Hidaway, and he agreed. "I'll be glad to take her on the farm, and any others you want to send," he said. We hoped we wouldn't have to take him up on that invitation any time soon.

We started looking at possible stallion mates for Audacity, and I liked an undefeated son of Northern Dancer. He had never won a stakes race, but Danzig had shown major-league speed when he ran. With his race record I thought he'd be worth $12,500 or $15,000. I approached an agent with the idea.

"Oh, you're really going uptown with that one," he said. "He's $22,500."

"With that race record?" I asked, amazed.

I thought about it for several days before discarding the idea. The measuring people ran Audacity against some stallions and came up with Transworld, an Irish classic winner and full brother to Protagonist, an American two-year-old champion. I looked at Transworld's pedigree and thought there was too much stamina in it for Audacity. Nevertheless, I signed a contract for a $10,000 stud fee for him. "Maybe we'll get lucky," I thought.

Chapter 5

As 1982 dawned, Audacity was at Hidaway Farm and Highland Mills went on training, enduring a long run of minor injuries, fevers, and maladies. Finally, in the spring it was time to send her on to the track. When I watched her train, she never seemed to be enjoying her work. I wasn't confident she would become a good runner.

We needed a trainer and didn't know any. Ed Stevens suggested one in Maryland, and Eddie Daniels seemed pleasant enough and competent enough, so we hired him to take Millsie, as we had now taken to calling Highland Mills. She shipped to the track in April.

Fragile Dream was broken and then went into training at Rocketts Mill Farm. She was beginning to grow on me. While Fragile Dream didn't have the best front legs in the world, she had a beautiful eye, with long eyelashes. Horsemen, I discovered, like horses that have a good eye, and this one did.

Yet, she really started to endear herself to me when she got to the training track. Unlike the first two fillies we had sent to Rocketts Mill, Fragile Dream seemed to want to be a racehorse.

"She wants to be the first one taken out of her stall every morning, and she doesn't want other horses to pass her when she's galloping," the assistant trainer said. That sounded like great news to me. Good horses — like all good athletes — have an attitude that tells them they're good, and this one seemed to be like that. My imagination went into overdrive. Fragile Dream, I decided, was going to be special, and I wrote that in the newsletters I started sending to the partners each month.

In June, Mom and I went to see Highland Mills work out one morning at Laurel, and she beat the other horse by better than a length. My intellect said that it was just a workout … it didn't count. Still, I thought it was a good sign. Maybe the measurers were wrong. Maybe this filly could be a good one after all.

Coming back up the track along the rail, Eddie Daniels was flicking Millsie in the face with a fly whisk.

"What did you think?" I asked.

"Well, she seems to have some speed," he said.

"Speed," I thought. "Yeah, her mama had speed! Maybe she's inherited that!"

As she got closer to a race, and as she got fitter, Millsie began to get more nervous. She had been high strung when we bought her, nickering loudly and walking her stall when Audacity was taken out of the adjoining stall. Now in the higher pressure of the racetrack, with all the attendant noises and new experiences and increased workload, she started to lose weight. The calendar reached the end of June, and the trainer called one morning.

"I'm going to put your filly in for next Tuesday," he announced. "I've done all I can for her, and I think she'll get a lot out of a race."

"Do you think she could win?" I asked.

"Well," he hesitated. "She's got speed, and that's good, but we'll have to see."

I had been telling everybody I knew about the horses for more than two years, and when I told them we finally were going to race our first horse, hands reached for wallets. Everybody wanted to bet ten dollars or twenty dollars on Highland Mills despite my telling them I didn't know how she would run.

"She's been training pretty well, and the trainer says she's got speed. That's all I know," I said. But that didn't seem to dampen their enthusiasm.

The day before the race I picked up the *Daily Racing Form* to see that she was listed as the third choice at 8-1 odds. I had trouble sleeping that night, and as soon as I got up the following morning, I checked the *Washington Post*'s handicapper. He had her at 8-1 as well. The favorite,

Bonnie's Friend, was a full sister to a stakes winner.

Mom, Sis, and I went to Laurel, all wearing pink, in some form, that matched our racing colors — chocolate and pink, after Winston Churchill's colors. He had been a longtime idol, and when I saw his silks in a color box at Laurel Park, where he had run a horse in the Washington, D.C., International, I knew then that one day I would like to pattern my silks after his. Sis was especially nervous. We had to sit through a couple of races before Millsie's race, and I decided to make all the bets for my friends. I went to the window and announced that I wanted $250 to win, $155 to place, and $105 to show on Millsie's number in the fifth race. The clerk grabbed his program to see who was getting all that early action.

As soon as the fourth race was over, Mom and I headed for the paddock. Sis really was nervous by then, and she said she thought Millsie would pick up on her feelings and become nervous herself. We left Sis in the clubhouse box, fingers to her neck, checking her pulse on an already hot afternoon.

When the odds changed for the first time, Highland Mills was the early favorite at 2-5. Like a lot of young horses, the filly didn't know what was about to happen to her. The jock appeared, wearing our silks for the first time.

Ten minutes to go, and the clerk called, "Riders up!" The trainer gave the rider a leg up, and Highland Mills pranced out of the paddock.

Back at the box Sis wanted to know, "How was she? Was she calm? Did she look okay?"

I told her that — to the best of my knowledge — Millsie was fine. Then on the way to the gate, she threw her jockey. We were instantly embarrassed.

"Why would she do that?" my mother asked.

I didn't have an answer, but the mishap gave us all a feeling of foreboding. An outrider gave the rider a leg back up onto Millsie, and the jockey steered her back into the group.

Then they put her in the gate for our first race. The distance was three-quarters of a mile, and I thought if she could beat Bonnie's Friend, she had a good shot at winning.

"They're off," the announcer called out, but I could see that already. "It's Bonnie's Friend up to take the lead; Highland Mills is a neck back in second." From the row behind me, I heard Mom whisper, almost reverently, "They said her name."

Bonnie's Friend and Highland Mills began to pull away from the field down the backstretch, and they were clipping along at a decent pace. The jockey asked Millsie for everything on the turn, but as it turned out, she was running as fast as she could. She tired in the lane, eventually dropping back to finish seventh. We thought it was a wonderful race. Millsie came back to be unsaddled, breathing hard and covered in mud. Our new silks were splattered with pieces of the homestretch that other horses kicked back at her as they went past.

"She'll do better next time," I told everybody. "With more experience, she'll be better."

Eddie Daniels said it had been a good first start. Now that she had some idea of what was expected of her, she could be counted on to make a better showing the next time she ran.

That theory was put to the test about three weeks later on an even hotter July day. When I arrived at the track, I found Eddie Daniels.

"It looks like a tougher race to me," I said, hoping that he would give me some encouragement.

"I'm glad you noticed that," he replied.

The race proved to be a carbon copy of the first. Millsie battled for the lead, running for about a half-mile and then stopping, finishing seventh again. Still, I found something good. The early fractions were much faster than the first race's. That meant that Millsie had run faster than before, even though the result was the same. I didn't understand at that point that she would have to run a lot faster to have a chance ever to win in that class. In addition, it was getting harder to keep weight on her. She was telling us in no uncertain terms that she didn't like what she was doing, but I wasn't picking up on it.

Meanwhile, Fragile Dream's ankles were carrying fluid. We had to stop training her and give her time to recover. And I was putting together another syndicate for the fall sale. This time we decided we wanted to buy a colt. We brought in a few new people and raised about $50,000.

With expenses split ten ways, the horse ventures weren't overbearing to any partner at that stage. Boarding the mares and young horses cost ten dollars a day, the training track was about twenty-five dollars a day, and the trainer charged us thirty-two dollars a day. The expenses were light enough that if we could get one winning horse, it could carry the weight of all of them. We had a contingency plan to sell Audacity's first foal if we needed to generate some cash flow. At that point we never considered selling any of the fillies.

Nine days after the second race, we put Millsie into a half-mile race at Timonium, a tiny track north of Baltimore. Since the purse was about half what had been offered at Laurel, the competition wasn't as good either, which suited me just fine. And in the half-mile sprint, we thought she could use her natural speed to her advantage.

It didn't work out like that. Three other fillies in the field had even more speed than she had, and they burst out of the gate and ran away from the field down the backstretch. Millsie was fourth all the way around until the third horse started tiring and Millsie got to her in a photo finish for third. When they examined the picture, it showed that Millsie had finished third by a bare nose. Though she won $450 in the process, I was disappointed. For the first time since she had begun her career, I expected her to win. She hadn't been close. So while it looked better, she really hadn't run better. I had the feeling that Millsie's racing career was going downhill fast, a thought I did not share with anybody else. If she couldn't be a decent runner, we were faced with two unpleasant choices: get rid of her and take our losses then or retire her and turn her into a broodmare. I didn't want to do either. I wanted to have a racehorse out there, running around winning races and money. It would promote my business. It would give us cash flow. It would show we knew what we were doing. If we had to retire the second filly we bought, that would mean the only possible runner we had was Fragile Dream, who was already having trouble staying sound.

Next we put Millsie into a race at Charles Town, where the purses were half of what they were at Timonium. It is an axiom in racing that higher purses attract better horses. The flip side is that cheap purses attract cheap horses. Also, we thought that with Millsie's speed maybe she could get an uncontested early lead. In that case she might get some courage and hang on in the lane.

Mother and I went to that tiny track in the West Virginia panhandle on a Saturday night to watch her run. The race was the last on the card, and by the time she was supposed to run, it was almost 10:30. The place nearly was deserted as we watched Millsie being saddled. Mother told me later that she couldn't help but think "this is the pits. There's got to be better ways to spend your money and time than being tortured at Charles Town on Saturday night." Millsie tossed her head and started sweating across her shoulders before she went out to the track, not a good sign.

The race was seven-eighths of a mile, and when the gate opened, Millsie took the lead. She led by a length or better as she came past the stands for the first time. Mom and I were out on the track apron, watching her roll along.

"Maybe tonight's the night!" I thought, and Millsie continued to hold the lead as the field went through the first turn and down the backstretch. When the horses hit the final turn, three-sixteenths of a mile from the finish, Highland Mills started running out of gas. First one horse went past, then another and another and another until six of the nine other horses in the race had passed her. She finished seventh, just like she had done in her first two races at Laurel but this time against much worse competition.

A rational person could look at her four-race record and see that Highland Mills was no racehorse. Horses generally get faster and better as they get more starts. Millsie was getting slower and worse. Driving home from Charles Town that night, I was silent in the car. Mother would tell me later that on the drive back she was thinking, "I can't stand this. I can't stand seeing my children so disappointed."

Almost a month later we entered Millsie in another race at Timonium. Her time off had done wonders for her. She had calmed down and gained weight, and we thought she had a good chance to win the half-mile race. It was steamy hot, but when they brought her into the paddock, she looked good. She wasn't sweaty or nervous, and everything was going well as they saddled her. Then a horse in the stall next to her began kicking the wall, and I could see Millsie's eyes get bigger, and she started dancing a jig. By the time the jockey got there, the trainer couldn't hold her still long enough to put him on.

"Just keep her moving," the trainer said to the groom. "I'll throw him on as you go past."

With the jockey up, they led her up the bridle path to the track. Going past some spectators, Millsie reached across the fence and tried to bite them. The jockey took her away from the other horses to give her a chance to calm down, and she went into the number three post position well. Mother had decided to stay down on the track apron, near the finish line. She climbed on a chair to see the race. She did that, she told me later, because she wanted to stand near the winner's circle and watch the race, so when Millsie won, she wouldn't have far to go.

The starters loaded four through nine, and when number ten balked, an assistant cracked a bullwhip behind her. One of the inside horses came through, tossed the jockey, and ran off. I cringed. Flipping my binoculars up, I saw the number three saddlecloth on the errant horse. It was Millsie.

The outrider caught her after she had sprinted a quarter-mile, and he took her back to the gate and reunited her with her jockey. Then they opened the gate, but as far as Millsie was concerned, she had already done all the racing she was going to do. She lagged at the back of the pack and finished dead last.

When I went back to the barn, Millsie was breathing heavily, her sides heaving like a bellows. Sad and disappointed as I was, seeing her like that made me furious.

"What are you breathing so hard for?" I said. "You didn't run a lick!"

I swear if I could have found a two-by-four, I would have smacked her with it.

I called the Allams in Kansas.

"Highland Mills ran dead last," I said. "Her racing career is over. She's a broodmare now."

Chapter 6

"Racing is a numbers game," people told me. What they meant is the more horses one has, the better chance one has of getting a good horse. At that point, I was zero for two, and with Fragile Dream's problems it was beginning to look like I might be zero for three.

Still, we had hope, and we went to the Keeneland fall sale with a new agent in 1982 with the intention of buying a colt. After a couple of days, we found a colt by a stallion named Hatchet Man, whose son Woodchopper had run second in the Kentucky Derby the year before. The yearling was a gun-metal gray with some splotches of white. We bought him for $25,000, even though his pasterns (the bones from the front ankle to the hoof) were a tad long.

"With a little bit of luck, I think he'll become a stakes winner for you," our agent said.

When we shipped him directly to Rocketts Mill to be broken, Ed Stevens wasn't that impressed. When we told him the horse measurers had thought the colt would become a stakes winner, he exploded.

"What do you know?" he asked. "Just what the hell do you know?"

I was amused by this comment, but my sister was distraught and angry. We knew we were far from horse experts, but we had been told — and we believed — we had bought a good horse. Stevens had a different opinion.

The fall rolled on. Highland Mills was shipped from the track to a new boarding farm in Flint Hill, in Rappahannock County, Virginia, hard by the Blue Ridge Mountains. The owner was Sandra Massie, a former fashion model who had an artist's eye for conformation. She was already successful in the breeding business, having bought her first broodmare and selling the resulting foal for just about what the mare had cost.

Sandra owned and operated Foxhall Farm, and she helped Highland Mills transition from her racing career to her new career as a breeding animal. She said she liked Millsie, but I thought she was just being polite.

I started looking for a suitable stallion for Highland Mills, and short and unsuccessful though her racing career was, it had provided me with some valuable information about her abilities. I knew Millsie had early speed but she couldn't stay the distance. I knew her family matured late and her temperament was hot. Therefore, I concluded I needed to find an early maturing, calm stallion that could run a distance. That's an odd package of traits.

Highland Mills would be sent to Kentucky to be bred because I firmly believed Kentucky had more and better stallions in whatever price range one could afford. I had no particular stallion in mind when I went shopping for Millsie, so I looked at the pedigree and race record of every Kentucky stallion standing in the $3,500 to $7,500 range, and I came up with one I thought was perfect. He had won at five-eighths of a mile and at a mile and an eighth, on dirt and turf, at two and three. His name was Lucy's Axe; he was a son of The Axe II, and he had everything I thought Millsie lacked. He was standing for $3,500. I called the farm and asked for a stallion contract. On Thanksgiving weekend I eagerly signed it and sent it back. There probably wasn't a person in the business who was as happy to be breeding to Lucy's Axe as I was, and as I signed I remember thinking, "This is not a $3,500 decision. This might be worth a million dollars."

This mare, unsuccessful though she was as a racehorse, was important to us. So was Audacity, even though she had never been to the track. We needed something good to happen, and we thought maybe the failures could turn into successes after all, if we bred them right.

We named the Hatchet Man colt Capture the Magic, and he and Fragile Dream spent the winter at Rocketts Mill, neither one of them doing much. We had Capture the Magic gelded, as we tended to do with all the colts. I wasn't impressed with his pedigree for a stallion prospect, and if I wouldn't breed to our own horse, who would?

At Easter we all were at my sister's beach house in South Carolina. Mother, Sis, and I spent a lot of time talking about the horses, and when the evenings came, we would sit on the deck and look at the stars. Whenever we saw a shooting star, we would make an immediate wish. And it was always the same wish: "Bring us some stakes winners."

The day after Easter I received a call from a vet at Rocketts Mill Farm.

"Fragile Dream has pulled her suspensory ligaments," the vet said. "Her racing career is over."

I set down the phone, shaken. The only horse we had that truly seemed to want to be a racehorse now couldn't become one. Just how hard was this game?

I went into the living room where everybody was and told them all the news. My mother put her head down on the dining room table and began to weep. The room went silent, save for my mother's sobs. I burned that image into my brain. I had started Bonner Farm with plenty of passion and a ton of dreams. Three years in, it had all been bad. Sitting there, watching my mother cry, I resolved to find a way, some way, to turn the whole thing around, to dry those tears and turn them to joy.

I called the Allams and told them the news, that we had a third broodmare, and I received the nicest note back from Bill.

"A bad beginning will make a good ending," he wrote.

In the early 1980s the horse business seemed to get wackier and wackier. Prices were rising constantly; and with the emphasis on pedigree over race performance, the value of a horse seemed divorced from reality. I went to all the sales I could, and it was hugely educational. One night I saw four horses in a row go through the ring, and the cheapest one sold for $700,000. I saw a man spend $1 million on a non-guaranteed breeding season to the great stallion Northern Dancer. Arab sheikhs began supplanting Japanese buyers as the foreigners with the most money to spend at the sales. The sheikhs arrived in Lexington in their private Boeing 727 jets, which were said to have gold fixtures in the washrooms.

Business Week ran an article about the booming prices, and even the generally stolid PBS televised a show called *Fast Horse in a Bull Market*. Naturally, an atmosphere that charged with money became attractive to neophytes who knew nothing about racing or horses. It seemed everybody and his uncle were syndicating racehorses and breeding animals, and their promotional claims were outrageous. The game was being portrayed as an easy way to get rich, and whenever that happens, one can be sure a fall is coming. When the market correction finally came, storied farms that had been swept up in the hoopla went bankrupt. I once met a guy at a party a decade after the horse market crashed, and when he heard I was in the horse business, he asked me if I knew a certain horseman. I did, though barely. He said, "I raised $50 million for that guy's horse syndicates. And he lost it all."

That's the kind of money we were competing against.

Audacity foaled a colt in the spring of 1983, and we had already decided to breed her back to Transworld, at a reduced stud fee of $6,500. We also decided to sell the colt at the Keeneland yearling sale in 1984. We needed income of some kind. After three years I didn't have much to show for my efforts, yet the show must go on, no matter what, and I needed to buy more horses. I found some new investors and planned my trip to the 1983 fall yearling sales in Kentucky.

Before that, however, my personal life took an upswing. While sitting in the shade of a tall oak tree, talking with a friend at a church picnic in Middleburg, I noticed a croquet game going on about fifty feet away. The picnic had started to wind down, so I stood up, debating whether to stay. Finally, I thought, "I used to love to play croquet when I was a boy. I think I'll go over and watch the game."

I went and sat in the gazebo overlooking the lawn and watched. I saw a pretty, barefooted blonde in a green dress skipping across the lawn, following one of her shots. She was winning the game easily. A brief shower brought everybody into the gazebo, and we all chatted until the rain ended. By then the party was down to about eight or ten people, and when the rain stopped, people said, "Let's play a game." The only problem was there weren't enough mallets for everybody, so we had to form teams. I wanted to be on the blonde's team as she had already won, and I wanted to win. And that's how I met Rita, the woman I married.

We started dating later that summer, and when I went to the yearling sale in September, I sent her a note every day, telling her about the terrific-looking colt I had found.

He was in the Taylor Made Farm consignment at the Fasig-Tipton sale. I had kept in touch with Duncan Taylor after buying Highland Mills from him three years earlier, and when I told him at the sale that I was looking for a colt, he said, "I've got one that you might like."

Duncan sent a groom into a stall, and the young man returned with one of the most beautiful yearling colts I had ever seen. The sun absolutely bounced off his chestnut coat, and he had white stockings on three legs. However, I wasn't so impressed with his pedigree. His sire was Cinteelo, a horse who had a reputation of having talent but being a head case when he was running. Cot Campbell had owned him, and during one stakes race at Saratoga, Cinteelo had refused to run when the gate opened.

But, I thought the scant pedigree could play to my advantage. The big guns wouldn't be interested in a colt by Cinteelo, I presumed, so I might be able to steal him. I thought there was a chance I could get him for $15,000, which suited me as I had only $40,000 that year. If I got him for $15,000, I might be able to buy another colt for $25,000 or so and double our chances of getting a good one. I was on pins and needles when the handlers led him into the ring.

The bidding started modestly and then began to bounce along. We got in at about $12,000, and when we had the bid at $16,000, I thought that we were in the clear. A long pause ensued, and it seemed whoever had been bidding against us had dropped out. Then someone else took up the bidding, and all at once it was at $30,000. I was disappointed. I thought we had lost him.

"That's too much for that colt," I said to the agent.

"That's our bid," he replied.

It felt like my heart bounced off my shoes. It was too much money to pay for a colt by a stallion like that, but he was so attractive, how could I not like him?

"Don't bid any more if someone tops that," I instructed the agent.

The hammer came down. We owned the highest-priced Cinteelo colt ever sold, I think. I gulped. Maybe I even went a little white in the face, but the agent had a response.

"If you don't want him, say so. There's a lot of people here who will buy him from you right now."

We kept him, and named him Allam after Bill Allam, who had been instrumental in getting me into the business. We immediately sent the yearling to Rocketts Mill Farm and started breaking him.

It turned out that we had outbid a big Florida pinhooker (a person who buys a horse for resale at a later date), and he came around to say how attractive the colt was and to ask if I were interested in putting him in his consignment for a Florida sale of two-year-olds. Duncan Taylor said the colt was one of the most attractive he had had for sale that year, so by the time my sister got to the sale — she had planned on us buying at Keeneland, a couple of days later — I was feeling triumphant. It felt so good finally to have a horse that everybody liked. Even Ed Stevens gave his grudging approval.

"Well, even a blind hog finds an occasional acorn," he said.

Allam looked like a star, and I thought we had finally bought a horse that would take us to the winner's circle after a major race.

Rita and I got engaged, and at Christmas I met her parents, who ran a restaurant called the Royal Mountain Inn in upstate New York. We hadn't told them at that point, and when we finally did, her mother jumped up and embraced Rita before turning to me and saying, "Now what did you say your name was?"

Their home and restaurant was about thirty minutes from Saratoga, a location I began to appreciate the following August when I went to the races there for the first time.

Becoming a married man made everything seem more serious. All I wanted to do was to make Bonner Farm a success, and I thought that I finally had the horse to do it. Allam was a gorgeous individual, shaky pedigree or not; I thought that Bonner Farm was on its way. Regrettably, matters didn't play out as we had planned. Allam went into serious training in February. A month later I received a call from Rocketts Mill.

"The vet thinks that Allam might have a paralyzed vocal cord," the assistant trainer said. "He's going to check him tomorrow. You'd better be down here."

"What next?" I thought. "What else possibly could happen to horses that we owned?" It seemed everything we touched in the business was doomed. A paralyzed vocal cord would mean he wouldn't be able to get his air. A running athlete that can't breathe is no runner.

I went down to Rocketts Mill and met the vet. The assistant trainer put a twitch on Allam's nose, and I held the colt as they put the spectroscope up his nose. The horse stood quietly, and I stood facing him, my right arm around his neck, praying there would be some hope. The seconds ticked by slowly. No one said a word for the longest time. Finally the vet spoke.

"I don't know … I can't see anything … Oh wait! I think I saw something move. Yes, there it is again."

The vocal cord was not completely paralyzed. There was some movement. I went back to Manassas, found my sister, and hugged her with tears of joy at our reprieve.

A couple of weeks later both mares foaled. Millsie had a colt and Audacity a filly. Bonner and I went to Kentucky to see the babies.

"He's not a bad individual," Tom Hinkle said about Millsie's colt, "and Highland Mills came through it very well."

The colt was a solid bay with a large white star on his forehead. While he was pretty correct, there was nothing outstanding about him. In the parlance of the racing world, he was "just a horse."

I had decided to sell Highland Mills, and I bred her to Faraway Son, who had been a champion miler in France and who had sired Waya, champion older mare in 1979. Normally when I worked on a possible mating, I would call pretty much everybody I knew in the horse business to get opinions about a stallion. I would mull things over and kick the idea around until it became clear in my mind. For Faraway Son, however, I really wasn't looking at the potential foal. Highland Mills would be gone before she foaled it for us, so all I wanted was for her to be pregnant by a stallion that had done something a buyer might find appealing.

Meanwhile, we needed a new trainer. Eddie Daniels had left Maryland for New England. A friend in the business suggested I call Charlie Hadry, one of Maryland's leading trainers, one who would later saddle a Kentucky Derby favorite. When he said he would be glad to take Capture the Magic and Allam, I was ecstatic. I immediately called my sister.

"We haven't had a lot of luck," I told her, "but I think this is one of the best days we've ever had in the horse business."

Capture the Magic went to Hadry in May and was off to Monmouth Park in New Jersey with the rest of the trainer's string. In July, Hadry called and said that our colt was entered in a maiden race at Monmouth. Jockey Chris Antley, the hottest jockey at that meeting, was scheduled to ride.

My parents, Rita, and I flew up the morning of the race. My Aunt Bunky — my mother's sister, who had a share in the horse — met us at Newark airport and drove us to the track.

The summer day was lovely. The sun and cooling ocean breezes mingled at the seaside track. In the paddock we stood beneath the trees and soaked it all in. I was pretty certain that Capture the Magic wouldn't win, but I expected him to run well. His trainer and jockey both led the meet, so I thought maybe we could catch some good luck.

Antley looked sharp in our silks, and Capture the Magic was the third choice in the betting. Our horse was calm enough as he went to the gate, and after the pre-race histrionics of Highland Mills, we welcomed his demeanor.

Unfortunately, his calmness did not equate with success. Capture the Magic broke last and ran last all the way around. Examining how the race was run, I noted the colt had been eighteen lengths behind after the first quarter-mile and eighteen lengths behind after the half-mile, but that he had rallied to finish *only* twelve lengths back at the finish. Making up six lengths on the leaders in the final quarter-mile seemed a good thing to me, and I was encouraged he would run better when he faced the starter two weeks later. Chris Antley again had the mount, but he must not have believed he had much chance because when the gate opened and the horse again broke last, Antley quit riding. Capture the Magic was so far behind down the backstretch that it looked like he was in another time zone. The official chart said he was "eased." Needless to say, his two performances left us deflated. We returned to Virginia in a state of despair. Here was another horse that was *supposed* to be a stakes horse, at least according to the people we had used to help buy him, and he hadn't finished ahead of a single horse in two starts. Pathetic. I was beginning to think that four years into the game, I would exit without ever winning a single race, let alone a stakes race.

The clock was ticking on whether we would sell Highland Mills. My sister was opposed to the idea, and my mother was noncommittal. I was the only one pushing for the sale, but I wasn't going to take action without someone I trusted backing the idea. Tom Hinkle advised me to keep her.

"She had a pretty nice colt for a first foal, and she's pretty well put together," he said. "If it were me, I'd keep her and see what she throws next."

I debated the decision with others, but then I called a man who had been down this road a thousand times before, Tyson Gilpin.

"I'm thinking about selling Highland Mills and wanted to hear what you thought about the idea," I explained. Tyson was quick to reply.

"Oh, don't sell that mare," he said. "Not unless you want to give her away. She hasn't had a chance to do anything yet. Give her a chance. She might be okay."

I hung up the phone and thought, "Well, I don't want to give her away. Her half sister by Seattle Slew (a two-year-old named Le Slew) might be a good one."

I decided not to sell Highland Mills then, though she was on probation as far as I was concerned. She had to prove herself to me.

Audacity's first colt went through the 1984 Keeneland September sale on one of the later days. Tom Hinkle sold him for us, and I actually was pleased when the colt sold for $7,700. Of course, we had paid $10,000 for his stud fee, $10,500 when you counted the sales tax. Still, I felt some exhilaration. I don't know why.

I was very aware of the fact that the 1984 sale was the last sale I ever would attend as an unmarried man. I had introduced Rita to everybody I knew in the horse business, and she had been savvy in a reply to a question from an agent I knew.

"Do you know horses?" the agent asked Rita.

"No, but I know George, and he knows horses."

Having never been married, I wasn't sure what to expect when I trod the nuptial path, but a friend had some advice before I left to return home. Tom Hinkle is a tall, native Kentuckian, and he speaks with a hesitant drawl that always reminds me of what a young Jimmy Stewart must have sounded like.

"Now, George," Tom began, "you're in your last month before you get married, and I want to tell you something." I listened politely to a man I had come to respect as a horseman. He went on. "When it gets down close to the wedding, you're going to be asked to do some things that you don't want to do … Just go ahead and do them. Things will go so much easier if you do. And smile if you can while you're doing it."

I laughed and listened.

Chapter 7

*O*ur wedding day, October 6, arrived quickly. I got up early that day and went to Laurel to watch Capture the Magic and Allam, who had shipped in a couple of weeks earlier. Standing by the rail on that beautiful fall morning, I soaked up the atmosphere and watched a couple dozen horses work on the track. I also counted my blessings. Maybe I wasn't successful in a game that was brutally tough, and maybe I never would be. I didn't know. Yet, I was doing what I wanted to be doing, and I appreciated that. I might have been making more money doing something else — or, as it turned out, anything else — but there are some things money can't buy, and the feeling I got that morning at Laurel is one of them.

While we honeymooned in Greece — Rita, a travel agent at the time, had found us a ten-day trip for eight hundred dollars — Charlie Hadry put Capture the Magic in a five thousand-dollar maiden claimer, the cheapest in Maryland. After losing to $20,000 maiden claimers and $10,000 maiden claimers in New Jersey, our horse was facing the bottom of the barrel in Maryland, and he responded with a good race. He rallied strongly in the stretch to finish a close third, beaten only by a neck. It was the best showing yet of any of our horses.

When we returned from Greece and I heard how Capture the Magic had run, I was very encouraged. I thought maybe he could win in a low-level claiming race and then go up the line, winning better and better races until he was in stakes races, where we still believed he belonged. Hadry said the horse's improvement warranted a jump in class, so we decided to run him in a $10,000 maiden claimer on October 23, my mother's birthday. Only my sister accompanied me to the races that day, and Sis went to the paddock this time, her well-documented nerves still on display, particularly because we felt we actually might win. As we watched Capture the Magic calmly circle the Laurel paddock, we talked with his jockey, Greg Hutton, who seemed confident. That was a first with us. Hadry gave Hutton a leg up, and Capture the Magic headed out to the track while my sister, Charlie Hadry, and I went back to the clubhouse and stood outside, behind a railing, at the top of the apron leading inside. We could view the track well from there.

I was able to see Hutton sharply rouse Capture the Magic when they left the gate. Two horses sprinted ahead of him, but our gray gelding stayed close, running easily in third as the field moved down the backstretch. When he didn't drop back as usual after three-eighths of a mile, I put my binoculars down and looked at my sister. She looked right back at me, and we communicated without a word that today might be the day.

The field rolled on, and Capture the Magic moved outside the leader. As the field turned toward home, Hutton asked our boy for some stretch punch. Capture the Magic responded, closing on the leader and then powering away. He didn't quit. He finished strongly, pulling away to notch the first win in Bonner Farm's history. My sister broke into sobs and fell into Hadry's arms.

"You don't know what this means," she told him, haltingly.

"You've got to get a hold of yourself," the taciturn trainer responded.

We headed to the winner's circle, hearing the cheers of those who had bet on our horse. After four years and so many disappointments, I wasn't sure we would ever get there. They brought Capture the Magic to us. We hugged him, smiled for the cameras, and quickly exited to watch the video of the race inside the grandstand. I had gone to Laurel for almost a decade and a half as a race fan. Now one of my partnerships owned a winner, and I was walking on air.

Sis seemed even more excited than I was. All the way home she pounded the steering wheel, exclaiming, "I can't tell you how happy I am! I can't tell you how happy I am!"

I spent the evening calling the partners who had shares in Capture the Magic, describing the race over and over to the eager listeners. It was the most pleasant day I'd had in the horse business, and — being an optimist — the start of something good, I was sure.

We bought only one winner's circle photo, and after having it framed, my sister put it above her desk in her small office at home. To the right was a larger, undecorated wall.

"What are you going to put on that wall?" Mother asked.

"I'm saving that for the pictures from the stakes races that we're going to win," Sis replied.

Mother thought that was the funniest thing and highly unlikely. Here we were, four years into the business and we'd won one race. And there was Sis thinking about winning stakes races. It was a comically hopeful situation.

Throughout the year, I always pondered which stallions I wanted to breed our broodmares to. My sister and I spent part of every trip we made to Kentucky looking at stallions. In 1984 we bred Fragile Dream to the good-looking chestnut Security Council, by the mighty Secretariat, for a $3,500 stud fee. He was a half brother to a couple of decent stallions — Stop the Music and Hatchet Man — and at that point, Secretariat had not shown he would be a failure as a sire of sires.

In 1985 Fragile Dream was going to a new stallion named Hyperborean, who was by a stallion I liked, Icecapade, and who had shown considerable speed in his racing career.

Audacity was barren in 1984 to a stallion who some claimed "couldn't miss" being successful. He was Nain Bleu, a French-bred son of Lyphard, a very successful and very popular son of the great Northern Dancer. Being a small, blocky bay with white stockings, he carried that distinctive Northern Dancer look. We liked him well enough to book her to him again in 1985.

For Highland Mills, the mare on probation, I decided on Nasty and

Bold. He had a decent pedigree, and I respected what he had done on the track as he had been in a very tough group that included two greats, Affirmed and Alydar. I bought a season for $6,500. For the first time I was breeding Millsie to a stallion whose race record I really liked.

On the track we stepped up Capture the Magic to a $25,000 claiming race on the grass, a huge jump in class. Charlie Hadry thought the gelding might like the turf, but others could see what I could not see: Capture the Magic was in way over his head and had no chance of winning. He didn't run a lick, finishing a bad ninth and losing by twenty-three and a half lengths.

We brought him back in a race on the dirt in early December and dropped him in class. Clem Florio, the *Washington Post* handicapper, picked him to run third and appended a note: "Poorly managed." The inherent criticism in that statement infuriated my sister, but deep down I knew Florio was right. I wasn't giving Capture the Magic a chance to succeed. I was so stuck on the idea he was going to be a stakes winner that I couldn't appreciate the horse I had in front of me. What's that they say about judgment? "Good decisions come from judgment, and judgment comes from bad decisions." I was making so many bad decisions at that point that I had to be able to make good decisions in the future … if we were still in the business by then.

Our trainer didn't help. Charlie Hadry was a very quiet, very competent trainer. As a racing fan, I had admired his horses as they always seemed to perform. Yet I never felt we communicated well. If he had come out and said plainly, "Your horse is a cheap claimer, and we need to run him in cheap races until we get rid of him," he would have been right, and I might have listened to him.

Later, after Capture the Magic ran second in a five thousand-dollar claimer at the end of February, we put him in another five thousand-dollar claimer ten days later, and he ran fourth and was claimed from us by King Leatherbury, one of the premier claiming trainers in Maryland. He never fulfilled the promise we thought he had when we bought him, but

I didn't help him become successful, either. In sixteen races in our colors, he had won one, was second once, and was third twice. Most of his losses were by five or more lengths, a considerable distance in racing terms.

Coming back only eight days after he was claimed from us, and taking a small rise in class, Capture the Magic was a closely beaten second; ten days later he won going away and was claimed for $6,500. We had owned him thirty months and had won one race. In eighteen days for his new owner, he was first and second, won $5,740, and was claimed for $1,500 more than King Leatherbury had paid for him. That's when I began to have a serious inkling I might not know all I needed to know about managing a racehorse.

That didn't keep me from making the same mistakes with Allam. He debuted for us November 24, 1984, running seventh in a maiden special weight, beaten thirteen and a half lengths. He came back two weeks later and again ran seventh, beaten more than ten lengths. He got the rest of the year off and returned at the end of May 1985 at Monmouth. There he ran seventh, beaten twenty-eight lengths. When he next appeared on the track, his odds were 118-1, and he lived up to them by finishing eighth, beaten by more than twenty-four lengths. The trainer called me after that race.

"I think we need to drop him into a $15,000 maiden claimer," he said.

"No," I immediately replied. "Let's see how he does next time when we run him on the grass."

It's an old idea in racing. If a horse is unsuccessful on the dirt, an owner never gives up on it until it has run unsuccessfully on the grass.

"Maybe he's a turf horse," they all say, and so did I.

He wasn't. He ran twelfth and last, beaten by more than thirty-eight lengths. Still I didn't change my mind about him. I knew he had potential. It was simply a matter of time. I never dropped him in class. I was stuck on a single convoluted thought: We needed to make money to pay for our expenses, but if we lost him in a claiming race, we couldn't make money, so it was better — I thought — to run him where we couldn't lose him than to face the prospect of having zero horses running. And he was so attractive that he just had to be a good horse.

On July 9, 1985, Allam ran one last time for us. He took the lead in the mile and one-sixteenth race and held it all the way to the stretch where two other horses passed him. He ran third, and we were joyful! We got a tape of the race and showed it to anybody we could cajole into watching. Of course, the fact of the matter was he was trounced by almost fourteen lengths, and in a field with some real runners in it he would have been ninth or tenth. But in our eyes he was finally living up to his promise, and I was certain he was on his way toward success at last.

He wasn't. I got a call from Charlie Hadry a week later saying Allam had pulled a suspensory ligament in his right front leg and needed some time off. Allam shipped back to Rocketts Mill Farm, and when he arrived and I saw how lame he was, I was distressed. I knew I didn't know a lot about leg injuries in horses, but I could tell this wasn't good. I decided to change trainers then and there.

"It has to be the trainer's fault," I thought. "How could he take this potential stakes winner and turn him into a cripple?" But, of course, horses tend to break down when they continually are put in races in which they can't compete, as Allam had been. In retrospect, I can see he wasn't much of a racehorse, and by entering him in races in which he was trounced while giving 100 percent, I had paved the way for an injury like the one he suffered. Charlie Hadry had trained stakes winners galore before he took on our horses, and he later trained the unbeaten Private Terms to favorite status in the 1988 Kentucky Derby. Allam hadn't been well managed, and it wasn't Charlie Hadry's fault.

To exacerbate the situation, we had bought Allam's two-year-old half sister that year, thinking that when he became a good horse we'd profit. Her name was Spruced Up Gal. Now, he was finished, and all of Bonner Farm's hopes were riding on her. And I needed to find a new trainer.

Chapter 8

We had started keeping the offspring of our mares in early 1984 and wanted to board them at a farm nearby so we could watch them grow up. I was impressed with Foxhall Farm, owned by my friend Sandra Massie Forbush, who had remarried. She was breeding for the commercial market and was doing quite well, turning a profit every year and boarding good horses for other people.

"Good horses have come off this farm," she told me and named a number of stakes winners that she and the former owner had raised on the property.

Sandra called me when the van with Highland Mills' 1984 colt and Audacity's 1984 filly pulled up, and by the time I arrived, the two were in a small paddock, acclimating to their new surroundings. Sandra and I chatted about how well they had traveled, and then she said something that surprised me.

"This is going to be a nice horse," she said, pointing to Millsie's colt. I knew and respected her eye for a horse, and, fumbling for a response, I put up a false front and downplayed the horse's potential.

"This is going to be a good horse," she repeated, "and he's going to show you."

So when I went looking for a new trainer in 1985, I called Sandra. She had reluctantly become a racehorse owner when one of her sale yearlings suffered a paddock accident one summer night in 1982. The filly was being prepped for a yearling sale when a thunderstorm rolled over the mountains. Lightning and thunder spooked the filly, and she tried to leap a fence. Her hind legs got hung up on the top board, and she scraped and gouged them so badly that she had to spend weeks in an intensive-care clinic in Charlottesville, Virginia. The plan to sell her at public auction was scrapped. A foot-long patch of raw-looking meat ran down her left hind leg. No trainer or agent would spend good money on a filly with a leg like that. Some vets said she would never run.

"You could almost see down to the bone," Sandra recalled.

After spending a considerable amount of money at the clinic, and with no positive prognosis for a recovery that would send the filly to the races, Sandra brought the filly back to her farm and simply turned her out for about a year.

"The filly was never lame on that leg, so I still thought that she might become a runner," Sandra remembered.

Sandra had tried to interest me in either buying or leasing the filly in 1983, but I shied away. I was having enough trouble getting horses that appeared sound to the races. I didn't want to hear what a trainer would say if I sent him one that had suffered what appeared to be a major injury.

Sandra had put her in training instead, and the filly showed promise. Sent to Charlie Hadry in 1984, the filly — named Nothing Sweeter — won her first start.

"I was flabbergasted," Sandra said.

Then the filly got better, winning a couple of allowance races, far better races than anything that Capture the Magic or Allam ever attempted. Naturally, I had been happy for Sandra, yet I was envious as well. Nothing Sweeter could have been our filly. She could have been winning races for Bonner Farm, and I needed a good horse badly.

"Geez," I had thought, "the horses I buy can't run, and the one I didn't buy can. I can't win for losing in this game!"

One day toward the end of 1984, Hadry called Sandra to tell her Nothing Sweeter was lame. He sent her home, but when the filly got off the van, Sandra saw she was walking fine. She called Hadry and told him that the filly wasn't lame.

"If you put some pressure on her, you'll see that she is lame," he said.

Sandra put a rider on Nothing Sweeter, and when the rider galloped the filly up and down the hills in one of the large paddocks at the farm, she showed no lameness. Now Sandra had a problem. She couldn't send the filly back to Hadry. He's the one who had sent her home. She needed someone new, and Tyson Gilpin suggested Barclay Tagg, a former steeplechase rider who was training horses in Maryland. Under Barclay, Nothing Sweeter blossomed. The filly nobody wanted became a stakes winner of $223,000. Naturally, Sandra was very pleased with Barclay. So when I called her in 1985, looking for a suggestion for a trainer, she immediately mentioned how pleased she was with Barc.

"The thing I like is that after a stakes race, he goes right back to the barn, takes off his sport coat, and gets back to work," Sandra said. "He's a real horseman." Coming from Sandra — who had spent a lifetime around horses — that was high praise indeed.

Tagg's success with Nothing Sweeter convinced me to ask him to take our two-year-old filly, Spruced Up Gal, and he assented. In the fall of 1985, my sister, mother, and I went to Laurel one morning to watch her work. In the company of two other fillies, she went about a half-mile, finishing second between the others. I was pleased. After all, at least she had beaten another horse, but I wanted to hear what Barclay had to say.

"What do you think?" I asked him, hopefully.

"Well, the one that ran third, I'm going to call her owner and tell her to come get her. She's never going to be a racehorse. The other one (the winner) is worth about five thousand dollars," he said.

Hmm, I thought. That makes Spruced Up Gal worth somewhere between nothing and five thousand dollars.

Spruced Up Gal never won a race for us. She ran second a couple of times in cheap races, and King Leatherbury claimed her in her fifth start for $11,500, which I considered a gift. We were in and out on her in less than a year, so we had cut our losses considerably. One thing I did note was that while Spruced Up Gal won a couple of races for her new owners and trainer, by my calculations she never ran as well for them as she did when Barclay was training her. I stuck that little fact away. At that point, however, we had no more horses to run. We hadn't gone to the sales in 1985 for a couple of good reasons. The people who wanted to be in the horse business with us were already spending their money on keeping horses we already owned: Audacity, Highland Mills, and Fragile Dream, and their babies. And I didn't think there was any way in the world I could attract any new investors, not after winning one race in six years.

In September 1985, we sold Audacity's Transworld filly at a sale in Maryland for $6,200. The stud fee had been $6,500. When one trainer took a look at the yearling, he said, loud enough for us to hear, "Her pasterns are too long. She'll never stand training."

By the end of 1985, we had one yearling and two weanlings on Sandra's farm. Audacity hadn't gotten pregnant the year before, but all the mares were now pregnant, so we expected three more horses in the spring of 1986. That would make nine horses we would be managing, which I thought was a good thing. The more horses we had, the greater the chance one of them might be a runner. But the flip side was that we would have nine horses eating money each month and zero horses making money. More and more I dreaded having to send out partnership bills.

Contemplating our situation, I saw that when I had gotten my family and friends into the horse business, I had thought I was selling them pieces of racehorses. By 1985 I realized what they were doing was investing in me. They all knew even less about the business than I did. They were attracted to the game because I had talked them into it, and that made me feel even worse. Month after month, in a seemingly never-ending process, I sent out the bills. To their credit, none of them ever complained. I was trying my best, but I began to think my best just wasn't good enough.

Yet 1985 did mark the beginning of some better news regarding Highland Mills. Le Slew, her Seattle Slew half sister, was winning races in California and New York. Trained by D. Wayne Lukas, Le Slew eventually turned into a pretty good sprinter, winning a grade III stakes race and more than $400,000. One afternoon at Saratoga I went up to Lukas' son Jeff, who was his father's assistant trainer. We talked about Le Slew, and when I mentioned that I hoped he would run her in the grade I Ballerina Handicap, he hesitated before saying, "Well, we'll probably run her in another allowance race. We like to let them get their confidence level up before we take on stakes horses."

I mulled that statement over. Lukas had learned from his father, one of the most successful trainers in the business, and his remark about confidence in the horse made sense. By 1985 I was sure that Capture the Magic, Allam, and Spruced Up Gal were not born brimming with talent, but I hadn't helped them, either. I had consistently asked them to run against better horses. How did I expect them to be competitive? Right there I swore to myself that any horse I managed from there on out was going to run where it could compete, no matter what level that meant.

We named Millsie's Lucy's Axe colt Highland Springs, after the high school my sister and I attended outside Richmond, Virginia. When he was a yearling in the fall of 1985, we sent him to Rocketts Mill Farm to be broken. To me he didn't look like anything special. He was a solid bay with a prominent nose, courtesy of Millsie. The white star on his forehead that had been so pronounced just after his birth had gotten smaller. Ed Stevens and his crew seemed to like him, but they weren't raving in their assessments. Highland Springs did his work and that was it. When we turned him out for the winter, we had him gelded. With his pedigree, it seemed clear to me that his stallion potential was near zero.

I had remained hopeful throughout this entire time, but deep inside I was losing faith. A couple of the horses that we didn't buy had become stakes horses, and we had turned down the stakes-winning Nothing

Sweeter. It looked like we would never catch a break. "How can it be so hard to win a race?" I used to say to my sister. "Horses win races every day. Why can't we win just one?"

Chapter 9

"Especially does history tend to underestimate the degree of suffering that the young feel when they fail. For at the time, the failure is total and looks as if it might be everlasting."
Brendan Gill, *Lindbergh Alone*

Anticipating all three of our mares to have foals the same year for the first time, Rita and I put together a group of twelve of our investors to go to Kentucky in mid-May to see the babies and visit some of the breeding farms in the area. We knew everybody wanted to see Secretariat, so Claiborne Farm was first on our list. Of course, Secretariat was the star of the show. We had a couple of spouses of partners who really didn't know much about racehorses, but they knew Secretariat. It always was such a thrill to see the horse that had set my dream in motion. I never grew tired of seeing that most magnificent animal.

When we descended on Hidaway Farm, Tom Hinkle and Mark Wells, the farm manager, were gracious and brought out the Nain Bleu colt that Audacity had foaled. He was a muscular bay with some white on his nose and on a couple of ankles. Like a lot of the Northern Dancer line, he looked like a sprinter, and we thought him clearly her best foal to date.

Next, Wells brought out Fragile Dream's tall and angular Hyperborean colt, who had a white snip on his nose and a coat that carried a number of whitish spots. He was surely going to be a gray before he got too old. We thought he was better than her first foal, so we felt that we were batting a thousand. Then, Wells went down the lane and brought Highland Mills and her filly out of their paddock. The three-day-old Nasty and Bold filly was very shy, and she tucked her head as closely into Millsie's side as she could. Wells took the shank and stood her in front of me. She was a pure bay, with not a speck of white on her. She had great soulful eyes. Wells said flatly, "This is the best one."

The weekend was a marvelous success. The foals looked good, the group was pumped up about their prospects, and everybody enjoyed the stud farms we had visited. We left Kentucky in a very positive frame of mind, but reality awaited us when we returned home.

The fact was we had no horses to race. Highland Springs was our only possible runner, and he didn't seem to be an early maturing type. In training at Rocketts Mill Farm, he hadn't shown any precocity. We thought he might get to the races toward the end of the year at best, but when he started doing some serious work, he bucked his shins and we put him on the shelf to recover.

No horses racing meant no income. Some of the partners were getting vocal. We needed to cut expenses, and that meant we needed to sell something. A pecking order had been established for our mares. Highland Mills — because of her improving pedigree and her three decent-looking foals — was our number one broodmare. Audacity ranked second and Fragile Dream was third, which meant she had to go. We instructed Tom Hinkle to enter her in the Keeneland November breeding stock sale.

Meanwhile, when September arrived, we sent the three weanlings to Foxhall Farm to join several others Sandra had. In the middle of October, she called me.

"You should come up here some evening around suppertime," she said.

"Why?"

"That's when the weanlings get running in a pack, and, you know, there's always one in front, way in front," she said. "I think it's your Nasty and Bold filly."

Horse people will tell you that horses are herd animals and that in every group someone establishes a leadership role. If our filly were the leader in this bunch, maybe that trait would carry over to the racetrack. Following Sandra's suggestion, I managed to get to her farm just before sunset on a cool, late autumn afternoon, and, as Sandra had said, the weanlings began to play and run together in a paddock. I had brought my binoculars, and when I focused on the leader, I was sure it was our girl. I savored that one image on the ride home.

Two-year-old Highland Springs returned to training in August 1986, and he really didn't impress too many people. He was methodical. He did his work and didn't show any feelings one way or the other about being a racehorse. A group of us went to see him work a half-mile one Saturday morning. A good work probably meant he'd be headed to the track the next week. We all stood in the infield at Rocketts Mill Farm and watched as he wheeled around that small track, Ed Stevens and I timing him. It took him about fifty-five seconds to work a half-mile.

Immediately afterward, one of the partners, Harrison Jones, asked, "What did you think?"

"He didn't show me much," I replied, resignedly.

The next day we discovered the youngster had bucked his shins again. If we rushed him, we might be able to get him back into training at the end of the year, but there seemed no purpose.

"Just turn him out for the winter," I told Ed Stevens. "It makes no sense to push him now. We'll get him going again in March or so."

When the November sale came around, Sis and I took a sad trip to Hidaway Farm to say goodbye to Fragile Dream. She was selling on one of the last days of the sale, long after the more attractive broodmares had been offered. We weren't going to stay to watch her go through the ring.

When a sales groom brought her out to us the final time, we both hugged her neck and remarked at how good she looked. The November afternoon wind was cold, and we huddled in our heavy coats. Here was a horse I had initially disliked, but who — because of her desire and courage — had won a place in my heart.

She shipped to Keeneland while we went to the airport, and I was silent as we flew home. I was hoping she would attract someone's attention, hoping that she would catch someone's eye, hoping that she would find a good home with someone that could look past her legs, her pedigree, and whom she was in foal to and see the wonderful animal she was. Sales, however, are pitiless, and the group of buyers still left after almost a week determined that she was worth … almost no bids. The auctioneer worked the crowd ardently before someone finally put up his hand and bid a thousand dollars. And that was it.

Tom Hinkle called to apologize, and when I got off the phone I sat down on the stairs in our house and cried. A thousand miserable dollars for a horse like that. That courageous filly had been humiliated in the sales ring. Unlike all the other horses we had owned, she really wanted to be a racehorse. The desire was there; the heart was there; the courage was there. But the legs to make it happen were not.

So I cried for her. And for me. Bonner Farm was finished, I thought. None of the partners wanted to invest a single cent in any more horses, and I couldn't imagine being able to recruit any new partners. Bonner Farm would sink or swim with the offspring we had bred, and when I looked at those horses objectively, I thought to stay in this business even one more year would require a miracle.

We owned six foals out of our mares. In January 1987, when they all would be one year older, we could show this group to the racing world: a three-year-old gelding that had bucked his shins twice; a two-year-old soon-to-be gelding by Faraway Son; and a two-year-old filly by Security Council. Plus, we had yearling colts by Nain Bleu and Hyperborean and a yearling filly by Nasty and Bold. Five of those stallions were abject failures. And yet Bonner Farm and all it meant to me were riding on the backs of these six young horses.

I was ready to quit, to admit the game had beaten me, but I was stuck. I had no choice but to play out this hand, to see what these six meagerly bred horses could do. I wasn't hopeful. I said out loud that I didn't care if I lost or not, or if I was through or not, that these were the last tears I would shed over my failure. Bonner Farm could disappear without a whisper, but racing was never going to get the better of me again.

Chapter 10

*I*n 1986, with Bonner Farm's fortunes waning even more, I got my Realtor's license and started selling real estate as an agent for a firm in Warrenton, Virginia. I liked the job pretty well, but I was hoping that it would be temporary. I hoped Bonner Farm would soon be providing a steady income so I could spend all my time in the horse business. I didn't tell that to the managing broker, however.

Still, I learned quite a bit about real estate and something else: about managing risk. I had seen the bubble pop in the horse business in the mid-1980s, and I was seeing the same situation in real estate in the northern Virginia area. I got more than one call with the directive to "find me a piece of property that costs around $500,000 now and that I will be able to sell for a million in six months." I didn't say it, but I always thought, "If I knew that, why would I sell it to you? Why wouldn't I buy and sell it myself?" By the early 1990s, prime location commercial buildings were selling for less than it had cost to build them a few years earlier.

While I was almost certain that Bonner Farm was through, I clung to a thread of hope. Racing is chock full of stories of bad luck turning good. Racing, you see, is all about hope for the future, and that's all I had left.

"If only we could get a horse that could win," I said to myself time after time. Still, I tried to put on a good face and carry on, though secretly I thought 1987 would be my last year in the horse business. Everything was riding on Highland Springs.

Barclay Tagg had consented to take him when our gelding was ready to race, and I felt good about that. People I respected in the game —

such as Tyson Gilpin and Sandra Forbush — said Barclay was a real horseman, and that was good enough for me.

Barclay is a ruggedly handsome man with sandy blonde hair. He leans forward when he walks as if he's battling an unseen wind, the result of being injured numerous times as a steeplechase jockey. A native of Unionville, Pennsylvania, Barclay grew up riding ponies and then horses, and when he quit as a jockey in the early 1970s, he decided to try his hand at training. Barclay met with little success before becoming an assistant trainer for Frank Whiteley, already famous for his handling of the champion Damascus when he got his hands on a streak of living brilliance, a filly named Ruffian.

"I used to ride Ruffian in the spring of her two-year-old year," Barclay remembered. "She was awesome. You could tell right from the start that she had something the others didn't."

Eventually Barclay decided to go back out on his own, and, like a lot of new trainers, he struggled. Without the backing of a wealthy owner, he hustled to keep enough horses in his stable to make a living. Finally, in the mid-1980s, he had seven horses, five from the same owner. Right before Christmas, she sent word to him: "I'm moving my horses to another trainer." Barclay was devastated.

"I had one pony and one old cripple horse," he remembered. "I was sitting in the racing secretary's office at Laurel, and Charlie Hadry saw me sitting there. 'What's the matter with you?' he asked. 'Ah, I just can't get anywhere in this game. I'm forty years old, and I work all the time, and I can't even get stalls at the track. And I can't get any horses. I think I'm going to quit.' He said, 'You want some horses? I'll send you some horses.' He had some owners that he was scared of or something, and he called them up and recommended me to them."

Being in the right place at the right time meant that Barclay could stay in the business. And staying in the business meant that when Sandra Forbush needed a new trainer for Nothing Sweeter, Tyson Gilpin had heartily recommended Barclay. Tyson, an astute judge of horses and horse people, saw in Barclay a competent trainer who only needed a break to show people what he could do with a good horse.

When Nothing Sweeter won the first time she ran for him, after a nine-month layoff, Sandra had been really pleased. And when the filly followed up that win with another and then a near-victory in a stakes race a month later, she had been ecstatic. But what really impressed her was Tagg's professionalism. It was clear that Barclay wanted to be the best trainer he could be.

Years of riding Thoroughbreds — he often exercised his own horses — had made Barclay a powerful man physically. He had the physique of an athlete, even into middle age. And, evident from my first encounter with him, he has a drive that is often misunderstood. He likes a job to be done absolutely right. He can't stand someone doing slipshod work around the barn, and he isn't afraid to let a person know, right then and there, if he sees something he doesn't like. He is quick with his ire, and it doesn't matter if the miscreant is a groom, a jockey, or an owner. Some misunderstand his waspish tongue for a permanent dourness. Years later jockey Jose Santos would question his agent when he told him to go work a two-year-old named Funny Cide for Barclay.

"Why should I work a horse for that grouchy guy?" he asked, and others in the profession felt the same.

Yet Barclay actually has a terrific sense of humor once you get to know him. He needles his friends constantly with a wicked wit, and he never lacks for female companionship. He loves his horses, and his barn is filled with stray cats he has picked up and cares for. His friends — of whom there are many — are steadfast. Away from the barn, he has a tenderness that many find appealing, but when he is working, he brooks no nonsense. He has worked hard for too many years. He isn't about to have his labors undone by someone who doesn't care as much as he does about his life's work.

Barclay and I didn't hit it off too well at first. I was put off by his direct manner, but I was impressed with what he had done for Nothing Sweeter. Under his care, Nothing Sweeter made twenty-six starts, winning eight, including two stakes races, and was in the money seventeen times.

When Highland Springs resumed training in March 1987, he showed more verve. In April, a flock of owners — including myself and other interested parties — made our way to Rocketts Mill Farm early one soft Saturday morning.

A bigger, stronger Highland Springs came onto the track that day, and after warming up, he broke off and worked a crisp three-eighths of a mile as we eagerly watched from the infield. At the conclusion Ed Stevens, who had broken all the previous horses we had owned, had an unexpected announcement:

"People of Bonner Farm, you have all been patient … and I think that you've finally got a racehorse."

We all cheered.

But having a "racehorse" is subject to various interpretations, so when we sent Highland Springs to Barclay, I had no delusions. I expected nothing exceptional from this gelding. He was by a cheap stallion and out of a mare that couldn't stand racing, and seven years of failure had knocked any idea out of my head that the game was easy or that stakes winners were as prevalent as shooting stars at night at the beach.

"You know what I want?" I told my sister one day in June. "I'd like a $25,000 claimer; that's what I'd like. You know, one that could go to the races and win and pay his way; that's all I want."

One day in mid-June when I called Barclay to see how Highland Springs was doing, I heard something unexpected.

"We're getting close," he reported.

"Where do you want to start him?" I asked.

"I think he's worth about $18,500."

I was flabbergasted, but I didn't say anything. If he could be worth that much, maybe he could pay his way. When I got through talking to Barclay, I immediately called my sister and excitedly told her, "Barclay thinks he's worth $18,500!"

We were giddy with that idea. Then something else hit me. If he's worth $18,500, why not give him a break? Let him start out lower, against easier horses. Maybe he could win the first time he ran.

I called Barclay right back and told him that he could run him for $14,500 if he wanted, and that's what he did.

On July 11, 1987, the Springer, as we had taken to calling Highland Springs, made his first trip to the post. In the paddock at Pimlico before the race, he showed none of the nervousness of his dam. Maryland's top jockey, the teenaged Kent Desormeaux, was on his back. I liked Kent. He was a dark-haired, good-looking Cajun with a fierce drive to succeed, and he had that confidence all good athletes have. Barclay had said that if Desormeaux were on any one of the top four horses in a race, that horse would win; he was that good of a jockey.

"Hey, brother," he said when we were introduced. We talked a little, and then Barclay tossed him up on our horse. I wished him well.

We went to our seats and arrived in time to see Highland Springs throw Kent. I could feel my stomach roil. "Just like his mama," I thought. But Kent got back on, and they went into the starting gate. A look at the tote board showed that Highland Springs was 10-1.

"If he can just show something," I thought, "Anything … early speed, closing kick, something …"

Highland Springs broke from the gate, hung around near the middle of the pack, and then just finished evenly. He was seventh, just like his mama in her first race, beaten seven lengths. When Barclay came back from speaking with Kent Desormeaux, he said that he and Kent agreed that Highland Springs had run "greenly," which meant that he was looking around and not paying attention. I didn't know whether Highland Springs would ever win a race, but I knew what I was going to do. I was going to give him a chance the next time out.

"Drop him as low as you can drop him the next time he runs," I told Barclay. "Let's find out what he can do at the bottom."

Barclay said that the lowest race that a three-year-old could run in was a $6,500 maiden claimer.

"When he's ready to run, put him in the next one that comes up," I said.

On Sunday, July 26, Rita and I went back up the road to Pimlico. Highland Springs was in the third race, a $6,500 maiden claimer at six furlongs. Maybe because of the big drop, Kent Desormeaux agreed to ride him again.

Harrison Jones, husband of Eleanor Jones, one of the shareholders in Highland Springs, was the only other person there to see him run. My sister was at the beach, my Aunt Bunky — who owned a 10 percent share in him — was at her home in New Jersey. And Mother, of course, was at home. I never thought to ask her what she was doing when the horses were running. A streak of pessimism runs through the females of the family, so I can only speculate. I'm betting she was at home thinking Highland Springs was going to run poorly, while subconsciously hoping one day she would be pleasantly surprised. So far, after years and years of racing, she had been surprised only once. But this really was the start of a different day. When we began, we were racing horses someone else had bred and raised. With Highland Springs we were racing our own horse. I knew what I was trying to do when we bred him in the first place, and I knew everything that had happened to him since.

It was a hot summer afternoon, and I was getting a big strawberry ice cream cone before the first race when Barclay walked up.

"If someone claims him out of this race, I think we should claim him back the next time he runs," he announced.

I thought his comment was unusual.

"He's beginning to come around," he said in explanation.

Barclay saddled Highland Springs, who showed some excitement, though still none of the nervousness that had plagued Millsie. Kent walked in, full of confidence.

"Brother, it's pay day!" he said.

That sounded good to me. I checked the tote board to discover that Highland Springs actually was the lukewarm favorite at 5-2.

Highland Springs didn't throw Kent this time, another positive sign. The horse warmed up easily and then it was time. I raised my binoculars and caught sight of the start.

Highland Springs came out of the gate well, and Kent sent him up along the rail into an attending position. He was running third down the backstretch, against a softer pace than he had faced the first time he ran. As the field wheeled around the only turn, another horse came up on the outside, blocking Highland Springs' escape from the rail. He was in a trap. He couldn't go inside the leader, and there would be no way for him to drop back behind the horse to his outside and then accelerate past the leaders. Kent was stuck in traffic, and, meanwhile, up in the stands, it all came to me as clearly as anything I have ever experienced. This was the defining moment for this horse and for Bonner Farm. Win now, win here, and he might go on to a good career. Lose, and he was on the way to certain oblivion. I felt sure that right then, all of Bonner Farm's future was riding on the outcome of that last quarter-mile of dirt, and there he was, trapped along the rail. Kent yelled to the jock ahead to give him room, but that jockey was trying to win and wasn't about to give the kid a break. Highland Springs wasn't fading. He was ready to pounce on the leader. In racing, it's called, "All dressed up with nowhere to go," and that's where Highland Springs was that hot afternoon.

Then — finally — the racing gods smiled on Bonner Farm. The leader began to tire and all at once veered to the right and opened a path one-horse wide along the rail. Kent asked Highland Springs for run. The big gelding accelerated through the hole and out into the clear. Now, he was first and running away from the field! Harrison,

Rita, and I stood and cheered him home like he was winning the Kentucky Derby. He moved away by two, then three lengths, his tail streaming out behind him. Now it was four lengths, and then almost five by the time he hit the wire. First! The first winner we had ever bred and raced.

I hugged Rita, gave Harrison a high-five, and shook Barclay's hand. We all went to the winner's circle. Kent got down, filled with unusual excitement, especially when you considered the nature of the race.

"You know how many runs he gave me? Three!" he said. "Every time I asked him, he gave it to me!"

We went back and called Mother, Bonner, and Sandra Forbush, who had believed in him from the start.

The two-hour drive home was simply marvelous. After such a long time and so many, many disappointing races by so many different horses, it was out of this world to have a horse win its second start. And he had won $3,300. I liked that. It was the most money any horse we raced had won in one race. That would pay for a couple of months of training bills. It might have been the cheapest race in Maryland. I didn't care. We had won! And there is nothing quite like that feeling.

With a win under his belt, Highland Springs began training with more fervor. We were in a bit of a spot with him, however. He had just won at the lowest level in Maryland, and the natural progression was to move him up in class so he wouldn't be claimed. Going against better horses — maybe much better horses than those he had just beaten — was something we didn't want to do just yet. Barclay came up with a solution.

There is a class of race called a "starter allowance." Though not a claiming race, it is limited to horses that have run in claiming races recently. Barclay found one on the grass at Delaware Park. The purse was $7,500, and the distance was a mile and an eighth.

In spite of the class, surface, and distance changes, we were hopeful as we drove the three hours to the track. Highland Springs was in the last race of the day, and he had the outside post. Barclay couldn't make the race, so he asked trainer friend Mary Eppler to saddle Highland Springs.

The Springer had a lot of support that day. Rita had accompanied me, and we met Harrison Jones there. My brother-in-law, Tom Young, also came for the race, though my sister did not. Mother was at home, of course, but Aunt Bunky drove down from New Jersey with a friend to watch her horse run.

As our race, the tenth on the program, approached, the already-thin crowd grew sparser; there couldn't have been one hundred people in the whole place. This was years before slot machines revitalized the track. Highland Springs had shipped well, and he came to the paddock and stood calmly under the tall oak trees. John Fitzgerald was scheduled to ride our boy, and — not knowing anything about this new jockey — all I could do was wish him well when we were introduced.

I checked the tote board and discovered Highland Springs to be the fourth choice at about 5-1 in the eight-horse field. I didn't know how he would perform on the turf course, but I thought he might be able to handle it. His sire had won on grass, and his great-grandsire had been an American turf champion. He looked like he might have the pedigree, but you never know until you try.

Fitzgerald sent Highland Springs right to the front, cutting across the paths of the other seven horses and securing the lead along the rail after less than an eighth of a mile. I had suspected our horse would show early speed this time, stretching out as he was from a sprint to a longer distance, but I wasn't ready for what unfolded.

Once Highland Springs got the lead, he relaxed. He had a short lead passing the grandstand the first time, and after a quarter-mile the field stretched out to such an extent that a couple of the horses already lagged out of contention. As the leaders hit the first turn, Highland Springs hugged the rail, with Just Monty edging closer. When they straightened up for the run down the backstretch, Fitzgerald let Just Monty take a short lead. I could feel my heart sink.

"He's quitting," my brain told me, "just like other horses we owned have done." But my eyes showed me the jockey was still sitting easily on Highland Springs. He hadn't drawn his whip. Meanwhile, the jockey on Just Monty was asking his horse for run. With a half-mile to go, Highland Springs easily retook the lead and began to edge away. I checked the competition and no one was making a move.

"Keep coming!" I yelled to Fitzgerald. "Just keep him rolling!"

Coming around the final turn, Highland Springs lengthened his lead, and, still, Fitzgerald sat chilly, not drawing his stick, not asking him for anything. He hit the stretch with a three-length lead, and with a furlong to go, he stretched the lead to five lengths. This race was over, had been for at least a half-mile. All Highland Springs had to do was to finish his jog to the wire, which he did, Fitzgerald's stick remaining down and unused. Another horse, One for Dom made up ground late, but at no point was the Springer in any danger of losing. He won by the easiest one and a half lengths imaginable.

I freaked out! I high-fived everybody around and gave Mary Eppler, whom I had never met until that day, a big hug that startled her. They led Highland Springs back to the winner's circle, and all I could think was, "He's won two in a row! Two in a row! We've never had a horse win two races in its career, and this one's won two in a row! And he did it easily!"

I looked at him and tears came to my eyes, which I hid behind sunglasses. Maybe, after so long, maybe the horse I needed was finally here.

Driving home, I couldn't stop talking about the race. I was jabbering to Rita, repeatedly going over the details. We had asked Highland Springs to get into a van and ship to the track. That's stressful. We had asked him to take a step up in class. That's hard. We had asked him to run a longer distance. That was doubtful, considering his dam could run only a half-mile. And we had asked him to run on the grass. That was questionable. And we had asked him to do it all at once, after only two other races in his life. And the thing was, he had tackled it all and won more impressively than in his previous race. This was a major achievement for our boy.

He also had won $4,500, making his total earnings for the past four weeks a whopping $7,800.

"If he could win a race like that once every six weeks or so, he'd win $40,000 in a year," I told Rita. "And that would mean that he would pay for all his training for a year and show a profit."

That became my aim. If we could just find a race like this every six weeks, he'd be the first profitable horse we had ever owned.

Meanwhile, the next ones in line, Royal Highlander (the Faraway Son—Highland Mills two-year-old gelding) and Marilyn Glen (the Security Council—Fragile Dream two-year-old filly we had named for a partner) were in training and proceeding toward their first starts. Already Royal Highlander had shown ability.

"He's better than Highland Springs," Barclay said flatly one day.

"He's got more speed."

That gladdened my heart. All at once Bonner Farm was on an upswing. We had a horse that had won two in a row in the barn, and right in the next stall was his younger half brother who seemed to have more talent. Racing can be good when you have good horses.

Meanwhile, Sis and I had gotten together to name the now-yearling filly by Nasty and Bold. We decided to name her after Mom, whose childhood nickname had been "Miss Josh." When we told our mother, she was less than thrilled.

"I can't believe that you all did that!" she said with a note of irritation in her voice. "What got into you two?"

I think she thought Miss Josh would be like the other horses we had raced before Highland Springs came along, the ones that couldn't run.

Back at Foxhall Farm, however, we were experiencing the first in a long series of hoof problems with Miss Josh. She had developed into a gorgeous classic bay, but when I looked at her front feet what I saw was distressing. The toes on both front feet were split wide open. Her hooves had cracks at least a quarter-inch wide all the way from the top to the bottom. Amazingly, she wasn't lame. The blacksmith patched them with fiberglass, and we started adding to her diet supplements designed to grow better hooves. We had decided to give her time to let the cracks grow out, so we didn't even break her that fall.

A couple of weeks later Barclay called to say he had found another starter allowance for Highland Springs. This one was at Pimlico, going a mile and an eighth on the dirt. The gelding would have almost one full month between races, and he was training better than ever. Barclay said he was becoming more "professional" in his attitude.

I had studied Highland Springs' family traits before I bred him. It was a pedigree in which the horses tended to get better with age. As August turned to September in 1987, that was a comforting thought. If he could put together a couple of wins at three, what would he do at four and five? I couldn't wait to find out.

The field for this race included some old stakes horses. A couple had earned more than a quarter-million dollars. Highland Springs had won the least, less than eight thousand dollars. He was stepping up in class and facing some tough horses, the kind racetrackers describe as "hard-knocking." All I was certain about as I drove to Pimlico was that Highland Springs was moving in the right direction. I didn't know whether he would win, but I thought he had a decent chance to finish in the money.

I arrived at Pimlico late that sunny, pleasant afternoon. I had always enjoyed going to the races there as a fan. Now, as an owner, I went into the number four stall in the little paddock inside that battleship of a place and waited for Highland Springs to appear. I checked the tote board and saw that Highland Springs' odds were hovering between 4-1 and 5-1. He was the third choice, behind North Glade and Blue and Bold. In a couple of minutes, in came Highland Springs, followed quickly by Barclay's assistant trainer, Robin Graham.

"How's he doing?" I asked.

"He's great," she said. "He's training better than ever."

Hearing that, I didn't feel nervous.

Third, I thought. Third would be okay. If he runs third, he wins $1,200, and that takes him to $9,000 in earnings in two months.

Kent Desormeaux came in, brimming with his natural confidence. We chatted easily, and then Kent and the assistant conferred briefly.

"He's sharp now," I heard her say. "He should be close to the pace. Just let him come away from the gate on his own, get his feet under him, and he'll bring you home."

"Right, Boss," Kent replied.

I was thinking, "This is great! I could be in an office, and here I am at the track with a horse that has a shot at winning a race. How bad is that?"

The assistant stayed downstairs by the winner's circle while I went upstairs to the outdoor boxes. The race would start an eighth of a mile to the left of the finish line, so I had a clear view of Highland Springs as he loaded into the number four post position. Only five others were in the field, so all the horses were in the gate within a minute or so. Highland Springs was fractious, throwing his head and giving the assistant starters a bit of trouble, but finally he settled down when one of them climbed up next to him and held his bridle. It was 2:24, post time.

He broke well, but Blue and Bold, on the rail, outbroke the field and took the lead. Kent placed Highland Springs on the rail in second, a length and a half in front of the favored North Glade. I glanced at the tote board to see that the pace was pedestrian. Blue and Bold clipped off the first quarter-mile in a tad more than twenty-four seconds and hit the half in forty-nine seconds. By then Kent had eased Highland Springs up toward the leader, and the gelding was sitting a mere half-length behind on the second turn.

"They're into the stretch now," the track announcer called out, "and Blue and Bold has the lead, but up on the outside, here comes Highland Springs."

I could not believe what I was seeing. Kent had Highland Springs in high gear, and he had collared Blue and Bold and run away from him. I glanced behind our horse to see North Glade making a run on the outside. Desormeaux looked to his right, saw North Glade approaching, and waved the whip in front of Highland Springs' right eye, just as a reminder to keep it up. Desormeaux had North Glade "measured," as they say at the track, and Highland Springs held on to win by almost a length.

I sprinted out of the box and down the stairs. Three in a row! All at once we had a horse that had won three out of four starts! Man, I was beginning to really like this racing game! And he had added another six thousand dollars to his racing bankroll. Now it stood at $13,800, and I knew I would be returning some of that to the partners before the end of the year.

I was the only owner there, and the winner's circle photo shows me and the assistant trainer standing by the horse, with me grinning as if I had struck gold. I spoke with Kent after the race, and he said, "I had this race at the half-mile pole. He had plenty left, too. That other horse wouldn't have gotten past him if we had gone around another time!"

"I think you'd better come and see this horse run," I told my mother that night when I called to tell her that Highland Springs had won. She promised to think about it.

Winning three races in a row — even though they were three minor races — put a spring in my step that hadn't been there in years, maybe since when the game was all new and fresh. Frankly, I was bouncing with glee.

When Barclay and I went looking for Highland Springs' next race, we had our first difference of opinion regarding him. I had found a tiny stakes race on the grass with a purse of $15,000 at Penn National Race Course, north of Harrisburg, Pennsylvania. When I proposed the idea, Barclay scoffed.

"I don't care how little a stakes race it is, it will still attract stakes horses, and he hasn't beaten anybody," Barclay said. Barclay hadn't seen the race on the grass.

"Well, he won so easily on the grass at Delaware Park …," I told him.

"Yeah, but that was against cheap claimers," Barclay retorted. "To be a stakes horse, he'd have to run in near track-record time."

I checked the track record to discover that Highland Springs had run in near track-record time. The record for the "about" a mile and an eighth on turf was 1:49 4/5, and Highland Springs had run the distance in 1:50 1/5. He was only two-fifths of a second off the course mark, and he hadn't been all out in the race. I thought he could have gone faster. Barclay and I went back and forth about this race for about a week until Barclay called to say he had found an alternative.

"Now, here's something reasonable for him. There's a $25,000 claimer coming up in a week at Laurel, and I'd like to put him in that." I consented. As a handicapper, I didn't think any trainer would pay $25,000 for a three-year-old that had been running for $6,500 a mere three races ago.

The trainer was also preparing Royal Highlander for his first race. "He's more talented than Highland Springs," Barclay, his assistant, and all the riders were saying. That sent all of us at Bonner Farm into fits of delight. We already had a horse that had won three races in four starts. If Royal Highlander was better than that, what did that mean? We weren't certain, but it had to be a good thing.

Race day, October 27, broke gloomily for Highland Springs' fifth start. It rained lightly pretty much all the way to Laurel, where my mother, my sister, and Eleanor Jones were going to see our horse run for the first time.

The track, while labeled "good," was coated in mud topped with a thin sheen of water. Highland Springs looked good in the paddock, as a horse on a three-race win streak tends to look. The gelding circled the paddock awaiting his new rider, Allen Stacy.

When the field went to the track, we made our way back to our seats. Highland Springs was 7-5, the first time Bonner Farm had ever started a crowd favorite. That made my sister even more nervous. She figured if he were that well regarded in the field, some trainer would claim him.

"Nobody's going to take him," I tried to reassure her, but I wasn't certain myself. I doubted it, considering the races he had won. After all, he had won three races in a row and still had banked less than $14,000 in total earnings. I thought it unlikely someone would pay $25,000 for him at that point, but stranger things happen all the time at the track, so I couldn't be certain. Still, Barclay and I thought he belonged in this race, and I steeled myself with one thought: If we lose him, at least we lose him trying to win, not trying to protect him from being claimed. I had learned my lessons. The previous years of losses had forced me to look at the horse's interest first. If I were a competitor, I certainly wouldn't want to be in a position where I had to run my guts out just to have a chance to win, and I wasn't knowingly going to put one of our horses in a similar spot. Highland Springs might get claimed, but would that be the end of the world? After all, in June my highest hope in the business had been to have a $25,000 claimer, and in October that's what Highland Springs was. How could I complain?

When the gates opened, Stacy urged Highland Springs to the front. He wanted to be the one throwing mud back on all the other horses, not the other way around. Second choice, Spouse Equivalent, went right with him, and the duo sprinted away from the others as the field swung through the first turn and started down the backstretch. Stacy had Highland Springs well off the rail, out near the middle of the track, where the footing was better, and he held a tiny lead over Spouse Equivalent. After a half-mile, Spouse Equivalent started fading, and Highland Springs had the lead on his own as the others sorted themselves out. Before we knew it, the horses were in the stretch, and Highland Springs had an easy length lead over a couple of horses that were going nowhere. Out of nowhere, the jockey on Uncle Ernie got his horse in gear and the late runner cut into our horse's lead with every stride, though his rally wasn't enough. Highland Springs won by a neck. Four victories in a row!

We all hurried to the winner's circle. Highland Springs appeared with mud on his legs and chest, but Stacy had on a remarkably clean pair of silks. After winning $8,400 more, our big gelding now had knocked back $22,200, a wonderfully pleasant situation. And, to top it off, he wasn't claimed.

There is nothing quite like having a winning racehorse, one that is paying its way and making a profit. The sun seems to shine a little brighter, the ordinary affairs in one's life seem a little more pleasant, and there is a feeling of walking on air.

"I smiled all night long," Mother recalled. "I woke up a couple of times, just smiling."

That was the impact that Highland Springs was having on my partners and me. The fall of 1987 was one of the happiest times in my life. Barely ten months earlier I was ready to quit, and now I was campaigning a horse that not only had won four in a row but also seemed to be improving with every race. Who could tell how good he would become? All I knew was that the cards seemed to be falling my way.

When an allowance race at a mile and a quarter came up a couple of weeks later, we entered Highland Springs. We weren't certain he could run that far, not with a pedigree that leaned toward success at a mile and a sixteenth or a mile and an eighth, but we would find out.

Highland Springs faced a rainy day and a sloppy track, and he never really seemed comfortable at any time. After contending for the lead, he ran a non-threatening fourth, beaten by more than eight lengths. I couldn't tell whether he didn't like the sloppy track or whether he couldn't handle the distance, or maybe he just wasn't good enough to handle allowance horses.

We retooled. He had come out of the race well enough, so we wheeled him back eighteen days later at a mile and an eighth, this time against starter allowance horses. He again caught a sloppy track; however, he ran well in the beginning under Allen Stacy, but then his saddle slipped up onto his withers. Stacy was able to stay on the horse, but he couldn't do anything but steer and pray. Nevertheless, Highland Springs kept trying, maintaining his position near the leaders before running an excellent third, beaten only five and a half lengths. Watching that race live and then over and over again on tape showed me just how far Highland Springs had come in his racing career. He gave his jockey everything he had, no matter the circumstances.

Royal Highlander was continuing to train well, but every so often he would do something stupid, like pitch a rider in the morning, refuse to go onto the track, or give Barclay's staff trouble when getting onto a van. We all hoped it was a passing phase.

In early December we entered Highland Springs in another allowance race, this one at a mile and a sixteenth, a distance more to his liking. He would catch a fast track for the first time in almost three months.

I couldn't be at the race, the first one I missed. Rita and I went to Florida that day as a part of a promotion for the travel agency where Rita worked, with all the staff going with us. We all shared a late lunch, but I had trouble eating. I was watching the clock. The race was scheduled to go off at about 2:45, and when that time came, I couldn't sit still. I was up and walking around the restaurant.

A thousand miles from where I was pacing, the weather was gloomy, but Highland Springs was ready to run that December afternoon, and when the gates opened, Kent sent him to the lead. He led the even-money favorite, Warm Season, by about a length through the opening half-mile, and when Warm Season began to tire, Kent let the Springer roll around the final turn under his own steam. Behind him the lone late runner, a horse named Entertain, was getting in gear. When they straightened out for the last quarter-mile, Kent pulled out his whip, took a different hold on the reins, and started riding in earnest.

"I asked him for his life," he said afterward. "And he gave it to me."

Highland Springs sprinted away to a three-length lead over Entertain with barely a furlong left to run and coasted in, winning by a length and a half. It was his most impressive performance by far, and the perfect way to end the 1987 racing season. The $11,400 he won ratcheted his earnings for the year up to $36,120, which I thought was incredible. Highland Springs had paid not only his own expenses, but also those of some of his siblings.

"An allowance winner! We've got an allowance winner!" I kept repeating when I heard the good news. I had started the year so low, and the first horse we had bred and raced had ended it on such a high note. He had started his winning at the absolute bottom of the barrel in Maryland, and he was finishing like a good horse.

As the manager of the syndicate that owned him, I was grateful for what he had done for us. At a time when we needed it the most, Highland Springs had come along, lifted our spirits, and had, quite simply, saved Bonner Farm. As the guy who had found the cheap sire and matched him up with our cheap mare to produce this winner of five of his eight starts, I was gratified my intuition had paid off. But with the fun and the victories and the vindication came something else: renewed determination. Highland Springs had saved my business, and now I wanted to take it to the next level. I had started the year hoping to own a $25,000 claimer and ended it mildly entertaining the idea I might have a stakes horse in the barn, though I wasn't certain which half brother it might be, Highland Springs or Royal Highlander.

Chapter 13

Owning racehorses is a roller-coaster experience. One day you're winning races, and everything is great; the next day the horse is injured, and maybe its racing career is over. People in the business have to be able to "handle the rough with the smooth," as the old English saying goes.

Bonner Farm had spent seven years in the doldrums, at the end of which I had been ready to give up my dream. Now, we were campaigning a horse that had won five of his eight starts. With a horse that consistent, I thought we could have a lot of fun. I think if you asked people if they would own racehorses, knowing in advance that they would break even — not even make money, just break even — the vast majority would say, "Yes!" It's exciting, it's thrilling, and when the field turns for home and it's your horse that's taking the lead, absolutely nothing compares. Frankly, it's addictive.

While we started 1988 on a roll, the year quickly tested our optimism. Highland Springs had taken about a month off and had raced again in early January in a starter allowance. Looking back on it now, I can see that while I thought he was an allowance horse, he wasn't. He had won the lowest level allowance race, and that meant to stay an allowance horse he would have to run against tougher and tougher horses every time he won. At some point — if he were to get that far — he would run out of allowance races and then he would have to go back to being a claimer or he would have to go on and become a stakes horse. Statistically, about three racehorses in one hundred become stakes winners, so a stakes winner is a precious commodity.

We brought a crowd to see him run in that starter allowance at Laurel,

and he was beaten at the finish, though only by a head. We were dis-
mayed. I thought he should have won, so I wondered what I had missed
in the makeup of the horse that beat us. Three weeks later we ran him
back in a regular allowance race, and the results were worse. As the 6-5
favorite, he didn't show much of anything, checking in fifth, beaten six
lengths. The next day we received the news: X-rays showed chips in his
knees.

"He needs an operation," Barclay said.

"How long will he be off?" I asked.

"Probably eight or nine months," he replied.

I didn't mind the layoff so much as its implications. At least now I had
a reason why he had run the poorest race since his first start. But that
meant he would be out of action all winter, spring, and summer, and he
had been the horse paying the way for himself and a couple of others in
his family. Now he was shelved, and there was no certainty he would
come back to the races as good as he had been.

Oh, well, at least we had the three-year-old Royal Highlander to pick up
the slack. The reports about his training had been glowing … with one or
two exceptions. He would work well and then throw in something quirky
— pitch a rider, run off in the morning, something. It was clear he had
ability, but he wasn't nearly as serious as his half brother. Jockeys who
rode Highland Springs would come back and say he was a "push-button
horse," which meant he would do whatever the jockey asked. Royal
Highlander seemed to have gotten too much of his mother's high-strung
nature.

We had our first chance to find out about Royal Highlander in January
when he made his debut in a six-furlong maiden special weight at Laurel.
He had Kent Desormeaux in the irons, and going out in the post parade
for his first start, he flipped Kent off, just as Highland Springs had done
five months earlier. I thought it might be a sign of good luck.

"Maybe he'll do a Highland Springs," I said, hopefully.

He didn't. He was trounced, running a bad fifth, beaten by seventeen lengths. Still, he was training well, and we did start him much higher in class than we had Highland Springs, so maybe he needed to run against easier competition to show his ability. Eleven days later we dropped him into a $40,000 maiden claimer, and he ran much better, showing speed from the gate, taking the lead, and then being run down in the lane. He finished second and seemed to have gotten the idea of what racing was all about, just as the Springer had before him. We were very pleased, and Barclay found another maiden special weight race for him two weeks later.

Going a mile for the first time, Royal Highlander broke sharply from the gate and contested the early lead. Kent Desormeaux sat patiently on him, and then with about a half-mile to go, Royal Highlander simply walked away from the other horses, as easily as any horse I had ever seen. Seemingly without being asked, he stretched his lead to ten lengths on the turn. Barclay was standing behind me and I heard him say, "If he keeps this up, we're going to the Florida Derby with him!"

Optimism from a cautious man!

But as the horses turned for home, I could see Royal Highlander shorten stride. With less than a quarter-mile to go, he was struggling. The other horses were cutting into his lead, which had seemed so formidable fifteen seconds earlier. A horse blew past him inside the sixteenth pole and drew off, winning by ten lengths. Royal Highlander was second, and I didn't know what to make of the effort. The way he had moved away from the field showed talent, I thought. The way he had quit in the lane indicated … what? That the distance was too long for him? That the field was too tough? That he was a head case and simply didn't want to run? I didn't know.

Regrettably, his next race was a carbon copy. The *Racing Form* had picked him to win, with the handicapper commenting, "Graduation day," but again he took a big lead and quit in the lane, beaten ten lengths again, while finishing sixth. I didn't see the race as Rita and I were in China — on another travel agent's cheap trip. While we were still there, the racing secretary at Pimlico hustled Barclay into running our horse in a stakes race with only three other horses in it. He ran third, beating the fourth horse by a neck and losing by almost sixteen lengths. He earned what's called in racing "black type," a highly prized commodity. "Black type" meant his name would be highlighted in a sales catalog with bolder, black type. Because of this race, Highland Mills' pedigree page would show Royal Highlander was a stakes horse, even though the distinction was a sham.

Royal Highlander never did live up to the hopes we had for him. We could never tell why. After the stakes race his back was bothering him so much that he was off for nine months, and when he came back, he won an $11,500 maiden claimer for us, barely holding on in a seven-furlong race. Kent Desormeaux, who rode another horse in the field, came back and jumped off his colt and went to weigh in. In passing, he told a trainer, "I wouldn't want to lead a single one of them back to my barn." Kent was right. A couple of weeks later Royal Highlander was claimed from us for five thousand dollars. The horse that everybody thought had so much more talent — and that had shown us glimpses of it — ended up knocking around in cheap races the rest of his racing career. He won $28,000 in four years of racing.

While all of the turmoil surrounding Highland Springs and Royal Highlander was going on, Marilyn Glen was getting readied for her first start, and on this occasion Barclay took an edge, though not something unethical. An often-used tactic is running a horse against inferior animals, especially in its first start. It means that a horse doesn't have to run at 100 percent of its ability, and it still should win. Marilyn Glen's sire, Security Council, was a recognized failure, and her dam, Fragile Dream, didn't even get to the races. Who would claim an animal like that in its first start? I told Barclay to run her at the bottom, in a $6,500 maiden claimer. As the race we had chosen approached, she was training better than a $6,500 claimer, and Barclay and his assistant could see that.

"She's better than that," Barclay told the assistant.

"Yeah, but George told us to run her there, so let's do that," she replied.

The morning of the race, Barclay was sitting in a car with Charlie Hadry, trainer of another horse in the field, one owned by Stuart Janney, the owner of Ruffian. Hadry said he didn't think his horse could be beat that day, then he paused and looked at Barclay.

"You're not sandbagging me are you?" he asked.

Barclay hemmed and hawed and denied even thinking of running a horse below its proper level.

I went to the races with Marilyn Glen, the woman for whom the horse was named. It was a cold, raw February day. It seemed like it might sleet, but Marilyn Glen the horse was quiet in the paddock and in the post parade, unaffected by the chilly weather. Back in the box, watching her warm up, Barclay said, "I don't see any way these horses can beat her." He was right. The race was a formality. Marilyn Glen ran like a far superior horse, winning without going all out. The announcer called out, "She's under a quadruple nelson," to show that she was being held so hard and still was winning easily. The human Marilyn Glen cried on the way to the winner's circle to see her girl, and we had a helluva day. Barclay had pulled a fast one, running a horse against the worst horses we could find and winning with her the first crack out of the box. The race carried a tiny purse, but that wasn't the point. Marilyn Glen had enjoyed her first start and won. Highland Springs had taught us that horses could win at low levels, gain confidence and experience, and go on up the line, running better and better. Maybe Marilyn Glen could do the same.

We jumped her up three claiming levels for her next race, and she ran an excellent second at a mile and a sixteenth. The race after that we pushed her up one more class, and she was fifth, though beaten less than three lengths. The next time out, however, we put her back down one class and she was claimed from us.

For some reason, it wasn't so hard to lose Marilyn Glen. She had performed well for us and would go on to have a decent career, winning almost $70,000. I liked the filly, but it was clear after running her that she wasn't going to be a really good horse. We needed horses that could pay their way at least, and Marilyn Glen was probably going to struggle to do that. Nevertheless, I got some satisfaction knowing that Fragile Dream had produced a winner for us after being bred to a nothing stallion.

Chapter

When I was thinking about stallions for our mares, I would question everybody I knew in the horse business. I would call a stud farm and speak to the stallion manager. I would talk with Barclay. I would write to pedigree experts and speak with *Racing Form* columnists. I would talk with Tyson Gilpin and other bloodstock agents. At the sales or the races, I would go up to trainers of good runners by a stallion of interest and see what they thought about the stud's offspring. (After we bought Audacity in 1980, one of the first things I did was to approach D. Wayne Lukas — whom I hadn't met — and talk to him because he had a decent two-year-old by Intrepid Hero.) And I would look at the race records of that stallion and any offspring he had racing. Most of the time, I had seen the stallion run. After a while, I discovered that the stallions I respected seemed to produce good runners for us. Whenever I had to be convinced to breed to a stallion, the resulting foal usually couldn't run a lick.

One person I wrote to was Seth Hancock, president of Claiborne Farm, where Secretariat stood. I asked him if he had a suggestion about stallions for Highland Mills. We had never met, but he wrote me a couple of long letters with suggestions for Millsie. He knew the pedigree well, as from Millsie's dam on back most of the sires had stood at Claiborne, and the last champion on the pedigree page, a filly named Lamb Chop, had been bred there.

I also talked to Tom Hinkle because we boarded our mares with him, and because he sold yearlings for himself and for others every year, he had seen pretty much every stallion in Kentucky. I valued his opinion and always sought his advice, though we often didn't agree.

Tom Hinkle is a tall, lanky Kentuckian who speaks with a refreshing directness. I called him one time to ask about a stallion, and his answer was succinct.

"George, I wouldn't breed to him if I could use Confederate money," he said. I got the message. That stallion was such a failure that he ended up at stud in Turkey.

I'm certain he must have scratched his head about some of my choices. Of the first eight foals we bred, only one stallion was close to being considered a moderate success, that being Nasty and Bold. The rest were either untried or unknown or failures, and the prospect of failure was something I understood. What some people in racing don't understand is that most racehorses are failures. They're failures as runners, and they're failures as breeding animals, and the more quickly one understands that fact, the more likely one is going to succeed.

Yet, just because a stallion is a failure with the general Thoroughbred population doesn't mean he will be a failure with every mare. The greatest stallion in the world in the 1980s was Northern Dancer, who produced a bit more than 20 percent stakes winners. That meant that four out of five of his foals were not stakes winners. Would you rather pay big dollars when you know going in that you're going to fail 80 percent of the time? Or would you rather take a flyer on a cheaper — usually lots cheaper — stallion you think suits your mare? For us, there was no question. We didn't have the money to breed to the proven successes, so we had to go with the cheapies. Breeding mares that were failures as runners — as all of ours were — to unproven stallions usually is a recipe for disaster. In our case, however, it worked.

When I looked at our record in the fall of 1988, I could see that every horse we had bred so far had gone to the races and won. To me that meant we had taken three lousy mares, bred them to stallions of our choosing, and had gotten better horses than we started with.

Highland Mills had won $450 in her racing career. Her first foal — by a $3,500 stallion — had won $36,000 in his first year at the track. Her next foal was a stakes horse and a winner. Fragile Dream wanted to race, but her legs wouldn't allow her. Now, her first foal was a winner. Toujours L'Audace had been unraced as well, but her first two foals both raced and won. We had sold them, but we kept the third, a little bay colt named Flying Scotsman from the 1986 crop.

I liked that entire group of 1986 foals, especially Highland Mills' filly, Miss Josh. Before she was through, Miss Josh would define to me what it meant to be a Thoroughbred. By that time, I was honored to have my name associated with hers.

The clock ticked slowly in 1988. We were waiting for Highland Springs to return to the races, and it couldn't come soon enough. Months went by until we finally had a runner, and when we did, it was Audacity's son Flying Scotsman.

By Nain Bleu, a stallion whose early hype far exceeded his foals' ability, Flying Scotsman was the most precocious foal we ever had. Barclay didn't think he was top quality and neither did I, so we decided to start him off in a $14,500 maiden claimer at six furlongs. "Maybe he can do a Highland Springs," I told Barclay, who agreed with me. It was a statement we made many times, after seeing the success Highland Springs had enjoyed in his first year. The Springer had demonstrated clearly that a horse could run in cheap races early on, win, and go up the class ladder. Because of our horses' mediocre breeding, we were able to start them off low and bring them up, if they had some ability.

My sister, however, was very nervous with Flying Scotsman's being in a claiming race. Bonner loved the horses better than she loved racing. She used to say that while I was the brains of Bonner Farm, she was the heart, and I think that's pretty close to the truth. She loved the animals as animals, while I wanted to see them win.

Scotty — as we called him — ran an even race in his first start. He stayed close to the early pace and then finished fourth without giving the impression he was going to threaten the winner.

"A good first start," I said. It was a better race than Highland Springs' first start, and Scotty was running ten months earlier.

When we wheeled him back two weeks later, we dropped him down one class. Now my sister was really worried.

"Let's give him every chance to win," Barclay had told me, and I agreed.

Scotty was in the last race at Laurel Park on a Sunday afternoon in late September. It had rained hard all day, and the track was sloppy. Rita, Bonner, Tom, and I sat in a box at the track and watched NFL games on the TV, killing time before we could go to the paddock. Finally it was time, and when the first odds were posted, Flying Scotsman was the solid favorite at 6-5. Sis never liked for our horses to be favored, especially when they were in claiming races. She thought if someone were going to claim a horse from a race, he or she probably would claim the favorite. While claims are made before a race is run, she still didn't like to have attention focused on our horse in a claiming race.

Flying Scotsman was unaware of the growing anxiety around him. He was calm in the paddock and walked out into the slop with ease.

"Ease" turned out to be the operative word for his race. He won it with ease, drawing off in the stretch to win by eight widening lengths. The others simply weren't good enough. We excitedly went to the winner's circle and had our pictures taken with Scotty and the jockey, Kent Desormeaux. Even in the photo you can see the tension on my sister's face as she scanned the track looking for a groom from another barn, one who might be taking Scotty away from us. Then Barclay's groom came to get him. He was still ours.

"See," I said to Sis. "You got all worried for nothing." She smiled meekly and seemed more relieved than exhilarated.

When I watched the race again, I saw Flying Scotsman in a new light. I was very pleased with his effort, and it seemed like he really was moving in the right direction. Barclay agreed.

"He came back fine, ate everything, and went right to sleep," he told me the next day. "It didn't seem to take anything out of him." Now we had to decide where to run him next.

The simple fact about maiden claiming races is that the winner rarely is worth the claiming price. Though the horse won, it ran against horses that might never win a race in their careers. The winner of a maiden race must next go up against other winners, and it's always tougher. A horse has to improve just to stay in the same class. So where did Scotty belong? That was a good question. He had won in a $11,500 maiden claimer, which generally meant he was worth about $8,500. The thing about Scotty was he had dominated the race from start to finish. If Kent had asked him, he likely could have won by more than eight lengths. So what did that mean? Was he worth $11,500? Surely. $14,500? Probably. $18,500? We weren't so certain.

"If we run him back for $11,500, they'll take him for sure," Barclay said. Obviously I didn't want that.

"At $14,500, somebody will take a risk on a two-year-old," Barclay continued. "We might get away with running him for $18,500."

I agreed. I felt relatively certain of one thing: I doubted he could win at the $25,000 level in his next start. We might keep the colt, but would it be the best for his career? I didn't think so. So $18,500 it would be, and there was a race at that level less than two weeks later. We entered him.

My sister couldn't go to the race, but my brother-in-law did, and so did Rita and a friend and I. In contrast to the last race, this day was sunny and crisp and beautiful. Scotty was in the fourth race, and Kent was back on.

Scotty was the second choice in the field of nine two-year-olds, behind a colt named Loud. Those two put on a performance from the quarter-pole to the wire that was worth the price of admission. Loud took the lead, and Scotty kept challenging him. The pair separated themselves from the field, racing away to a ten-length lead over the horse running third. Inside the last hundred yards, Scotty was at Loud's neck, then his nose, and when they flashed past the wire, it was too close to call.

We were wrung out from yelling, and when we watched the slow-motion replay, it seemed to me that Loud had won. Flying Scotsman and Loud circled outside the winner's circle, waiting for the stewards to examine the photo and determine the winner. Whether he had won or not, I was extremely happy with his performance. Scotty had tried hard all the way down the lane, never giving an inch.

Then … we won! The photo showed Flying Scotsman by maybe an inch. We rushed enthusiastically to the winner's circle, bursting with pride over his performance.

"He kept digging and digging and digging," an excited Kent Desormeaux related. "I didn't touch him with the whip, he was trying so hard by himself, I didn't want to throw him off stride."

Barclay was pleased, and I was ecstatic. It seemed Flying Scotsman really did have a future.

"He might be the next Highland Springs," I said to no one, and then … someone different arrived to take him out of the winner's circle. He had been claimed from us. Talk about going from the highest high to the lowest low in the span of a few seconds — that's what happened to us.

The ride home that afternoon was a solemn one. I kept playing the decision to run him for that price over and over in my mind, and at the end I was certain I had done the right thing. After all, he had won by only a nose. One class higher and he surely would have lost. Tactically, it was the right decision, but the little colt had won me over with his pluckiness, and I was sad to see him go. My sister was so attached to him that when he ran later for someone else, she went to the track to see him run. I think she even introduced herself to the new owners and went to the winner's circle with them.

It turned out the sadness from losing Scotty was brief. Two days later Highland Springs returned to the races.

Chapter 15

Highland Springs had been training well for about three months, and Barclay chose an allowance race for the gelding's first start back. The distance was seven furlongs, shorter than he was used to running, but we were more concerned with finding out whether he was the same horse rather than with winning that specific race.

"I think he'll do okay," Barclay had told me when he announced the plan, and I hoped that was true, but I didn't expect him to win. Not at that distance. Not after an operation and an eight-and-a-half-month layoff. In addition, the Springer had a new jockey, Donnie Miller. Barclay thought he would suit the horse.

"He's a quiet rider, and Highland Springs doesn't want a lot of whooping and hollering, so I think he'll be fine," he said.

Race day found every owner some place other than at the track. We were all out of town for one reason or the other, but I called in as soon as I felt the race would be official.

"Who won the ninth race?" I asked the clerk in the racing secretary's office.

"Highland Springs," he said, without emotion.

"Thank you," I said quietly, and then I hung up the phone and let out a yell that startled Rita.

"He won it, baby! He won it!"

The video of the race was even better. It showed the Springer taking the lead coming right out of the gate, warding off one horse after another, and drawing away to win by a length and change. He was the longest shot in the field; a two-dollar win bet paid a whopping $26.20. I was gleeful, especially when I looked at the racing figures I kept. They showed that — off a ten-month layoff — he had run a better race than any the year before.

The Springer earned $15,600 for his victory, taking his total earnings to more than $50,000, and he came back fine. He was ready to roll again a mere seventeen days later in another allowance race, but this one was at a mile and one-eighth on the grass.

It was his first time back on the turf since his easy victory fourteen months earlier, and fans noted his current form and his back class on the turf. He was made the 2-1 favorite, and he ran like a favorite should, toying with the field and winning under wraps. He had won two grass races without being tested, a fact that would become more important in the months ahead. He was back at it again seventeen days later, this time on the dirt, and this time he ran a close second in another allowance race. A week later he blitzed the field in a nine-furlong dirt race, accelerating into a headwind that blew Donnie Miller's cap off his helmet. From four races in six weeks, Highland Springs had won almost $50,000, and it was clear to all that he had gotten better with age, a family trait.

We ran into Miller that evening in a local restaurant and congratulated him again on his ride.

"It was easy," he said. "All I had to do was steer."

All at once it hit me. We had reached the stage I had thought about almost a year earlier. Highland Springs had reached the point at which he either had to face higher-quality horses or run against claiming company. He had practically run out of allowance races.

Still training well, Highland Springs gave every impression he deserved a shot at a stakes race, so Barclay aimed him at one coming up at Laurel on December 11, the same day we had Royal Highlander running at the same place.

Royal Highlander was in the first race, and Highland Springs was in the ninth, the mile and an eighth Walter Haight Handicap. That meant that we had to get there early and wait through the whole day, gradually getting more and more nervous.

Royal Highlander did his part, struggling to his only win for us. Afterward, we called Mom, who was in the hospital recovering from cancer surgery.

"He won," I said matter-of-factly. "We're half-way to a great day."

The Springer looked good, but in spite of his recent record, the bettors didn't think much of his chances. They sent him off at 14-1. The favorite was Little Bold John, a Maryland institution who had won more than a million dollars in his career. Donnie Miller abandoned Highland Springs to stay with Little Bold John, as well he should. Allen Stacy, who had ridden the Springer the previous year, was back aboard.

After climbing the stairs back to our seats to watch the race, I turned to Barclay.

"Win, lose, or draw, thanks for getting us to this point," I told him. I was certain that in other hands Highland Springs would have ended up a cheap claimer at a little track somewhere. Barclay had stayed with him, worked hard with him, and had given him every opportunity to become a good horse. With his pedigree and his early race record, I think that other trainers would have used Highland Springs up and discarded him before he had his shot. Now, he was a winner of nearly $90,000, and he was in a stakes race, a phenomenal climb from the $6,500 maiden claimer where he had his first win.

Highland Springs rallied to the lead on the turn for home, but he held it for a couple of seconds at most. A horde of horses soon rallied past him, with Balthazar B. running away to win and Little Bold John second. The Springer checked in sixth, beaten more than fifteen lengths. Looking at the results, someone could judge that Highland Springs was no stakes horse, which meant that he was going into the claiming ranks. We ran him back in a $75,000 claimer at Laurel four weeks later, and he was a bad fourth in the mud, beaten by more than thirteen lengths.

After that race we decided to give him some time off. The weather was lousy — it being the dead of winter — and he wasn't performing well.

Better to take the time to let him recapture his form.

Hanging over the discussion, though unsaid at the time, was the thought that maybe he was finished. I didn't say anything to anybody, but I could see that running on the dirt, at least, he was on a downward slope.

But the nice thing, as 1988 turned into 1989, was that Miss Josh was getting ready to go to the races.

I called the barn one day before the stakes race in December to inquire about Highland Springs and the others we had there. For the first time, I could say something that I had wanted to say since before I entered the business:

"How's the big horse?" I asked of the assistant trainer.

The "big horse" around a barn is the leader of the pack. It's the one that makes the trainer and the staff want to get up and go to the barn every day. Stakes horses are called big horses, and if a trainer is lucky and the barn is filled with stakes winners, the biggest winner of the bunch or the one that has won the most impressive races is known as the big horse. When I called the barn that morning, Highland Springs was the only horse in Barclay's barn close to being a stakes horse. Calling him the big horse was a little joke on my part. He hadn't done enough to gain that title. What I didn't expect was the answer.

"Which one?" Robin Graham replied.

"What do you mean?" I came right back.

"I mean that Miss Josh is training awfully well," she said. "Maybe you've got another big horse."

There are moments in any business when you want to shout out for joy, and that was one for me. At the end of the conversation, I put down the phone and whooped. Could it be possible that we might have another good horse? I floated happily through the rest of the day.

Chapter 16

By the beginning of 1989, Royal Highlander was gone, Flying Scotsman was gone, and Marilyn Glen was long gone — all claimed away. Highland Springs had run dismally in the mud at Laurel on January 8 and seemed to be drifting lower in class. Still, we had a couple of unraced three-year-olds — Winds of Change (Fragile Dream's last foal for us) and Miss Josh, whose racing career I looked forward to.

Rita and I also discovered we were going to be parents. The baby was due the beginning of September. Naturally, like other first-time parents-to-be, we were happy with anticipation.

On the equine front Highland Mills was in foal to Vigors who, during his racing career, had a couple of cool nicknames. Some called him White Lightning, while others called him the White Tornado, due to the color of his coat and the terrific burst of energy with which he finished races. I thought he was the best stallion we had bred Millsie to.

We didn't know what to expect from either Winds of Change or Miss Josh. As much as I liked Miss Josh, she did have some physical problems. Primarily, the main problem was with her feet. The old saying in racing is "No hoof, no horse," which means that if a horse's hooves bother it, the horse is not likely to want to run fast enough to win. Miss Josh's feet were below average. They were small for a horse her size, flat, and thin soled. When she was a yearling, she developed splits a quarter-inch wide in both front hooves. From time to time they kept her off the track while she recovered from some lameness. Yet, for the most part, she soldiered on.

Her career didn't get off to a promising start. With her pedigree, which was pretty light at that stage, and her feet, we felt certain nobody would claim her in maiden claiming races.

She ran first in a $50,000 maiden claimer on March 10 at Pimlico, and the track surface was absolutely terrible, a sloppy mess. Miss Josh couldn't find her footing at all, and she checked in dead last, beaten by almost nineteen lengths. We ran her back three and a half weeks later at Laurel Park and dropped her in class to a $25,000 maiden claimer, but that didn't help much. She was sixth, beaten by less than four lengths. Five weeks later we put her in a $16,000 maiden claimer, and she was fifth, beaten by six lengths. It seemed her career was almost finished before it even started. Barclay and I went to the video room afterward to watch the race tape to see if we could find some plausible reason she had run so poorly. We couldn't find one.

"I wouldn't want a single one of those fillies," said another trainer who was there as we watched all angles and all views.

Barclay jerked his thumb toward me and said, "Here's the owner of the one that ran fifth."

The other trainer jumped up, all embarrassed, and said, "Oh, I'm sorry! I didn't mean anything by it." I was more amused than anything else. He was entitled to his opinion, and, on the surface at least, he seemed right. Miss Josh had done nothing to distinguish herself.

In a last-ditch effort to try and help a filly I loved win a race, we decided to drop her in class once again, to a $12,000 maiden claimer and run her back in a few weeks.

In the meantime, Winds of Change made his first start on April 28 in a $25,000 maiden claimer at Pimlico. Because of work commitments at my job in real estate, I couldn't attend the race, and afterward I was shocked to hear he had run seventh and had been claimed.

"What could anyone possibly have seen in him to take him first time out?" I asked assistant trainer Robin Graham. She volunteered that maybe someone took him based on a good workout the *Racing Form* had listed. That was tough to take, even though we were better off financially with the $25,000. He went on to earn $83,000 over a long, undistinguished career.

When Highland Springs returned to the track in April, he ran badly in a $60,000 six-furlong claimer at Pimlico, beaten by about fourteen lengths in the slop. I called Barclay a few days later, and he and I talked about Highland Springs and Miss Josh.

"I think that you'd better consider dropping both of them down and getting rid of them," he advised. I made no commitments. Having seen both of Highland Springs' turf races, I refused to believe the Springer was finished as a racehorse until I saw him run badly on the grass.

At the end of May, my mother, sister, brother-in-law, father, and some others went to Kentucky to see Highland Mills' latest foal, a gray colt. He was good-sized, with a frame that seemed to indicate he was going to be big. And he had an attitude, even at two weeks old. While my sister was leaning on the fence of his paddock, he leaned back and kicked at her. His hoof hit the board under her head, scaring the hell out of her. I liked that. I always liked a horse with spirit.

While we were in Kentucky, Barclay entered Highland Springs in an allowance race at Delaware Park. The purse was a paltry $9,500, but the race was a mile on the grass. We flew home from Kentucky, got in the car at the airport, and drove right to Delaware. Overnight rain caused the race to be taken off the grass, so the Springer was going to run on the dirt. When he came to the paddock, I saw something I had never seen in him before. He was stone-cold scared. He was so frightened that his knees shook. Barclay had said a couple of times that the horse was a nervous sort, but that "it's on the inside. He doesn't show it on the outside." Today it had worked its way to the surface.

His condition tipped us off to how he would run, which was below par. In that tiny race, he finished third, beaten almost eight lengths. Driving home, all of us were quiet. Our first good horse seemed to have come to the end of the line.

"You really like this?" my sister asked after the race, a tone of incredulity in her voice. "You really like racing?" She had never liked the competition. She most preferred being around the animals, especially the babies.

"Yes," I replied. It had taken me a long time to get to the point where I could even have a racehorse and even longer to get a winner. In spite of the fact that Highland Springs seemed close to the end of his career, I was happy to be in the game. And I still wanted to see him run on the grass. All he had shown me was that he couldn't cut it on the dirt anymore.

The calendar tipped over into June, and all at once our racing fortunes took a gigantic turn for the better. Miss Josh started in a $12,000 maiden claimer at Pimlico on June 2 and, under Kent Desormeaux, walloped the field, winning by seven lengths. I was the only one there to see her win, and cheap race or not, I was very proud of my girl.

Two days later Highland Springs got his chance to prove me right or wrong. Barclay wheeled him back into a $35,000 claimer on the grass at Pimlico. This was it. Once again, Highland Spring's future was riding on one race. He had been the moneymaker for us for two years, but through the first five months of 1989 he had banked a measly $2,700. He needed a win badly.

I wasn't at Pimlico to see the race. I was in Colorado at a family wedding, but I got on the phone to the track as soon as I could afterward.

"Who won the fourth race?" I queried, holding my breath. I could feel my heart beat as the man in the racing secretary's office went to check. Thirty seconds later — it seemed a decade — he came back on the phone to say flatly, "Highland Springs."

"Was he claimed?" I asked, now really sweating it.

"Nope," he replied.

I hung up and let out a war whoop. A winner again, and still ours! When I saw the tape of the race, I felt even better. He had dominated the field, winning easily by four. Race announcer Trevor Denman — on sabbatical from the California tracks — called out as Highland Springs turned for home, "Donnie Miller cocks his stick, but he knows he's going too well for this field … Highland Springs by eight lengths at the sixteenth pole!"

I knew what I wanted to do with Highland Springs next. I thought he was a streaky runner, putting his good races together in bunches. If that were true, I wanted to go into a stakes race next time out, which represented a massive jump in class. I nominated him to the Chieftain Handicap, a mile and a sixteenth on the turf, two weeks later at Pimlico. Barclay was reluctant.

"There's a $100,000 claimer on the grass in ten days," he advised. "Let's put him in that, and if he wins, then we can come back in a stakes race."

I probably would have gone along with that idea, but it didn't bother me too much when the race didn't get enough horses to fill. Now we had no alternative but the Chieftain Handicap.

Miss Josh returned to the track for her next start, a $20,000 six-furlong claimer, nine days after the Springer won. My brother-in-law and I went to the race, and we met up with Barclay before our filly came to the paddock. It was June 13, just days after the Triple Crown races had been completed for that year, and amid some idle chit-chat, a thought came to me.

"You know, Barclay, I looked at those trainers with horses in the Triple Crown, and I know that you can train a good horse to run in a big race," I said.

Barclay seemed a tad stunned. He looked quizzically at me but said nothing.

I meant it. I had grown to admire Barclay. I had known him four years by then and had seen his work ethic, his demanding ways, and his intolerance for the slapdash. We had known success with him that we wouldn't have with many other trainers. Of that, I was certain. We might never have the wherewithal to buy him a stable full of expensive yearlings, but I was sure he would get the best out of any horse we sent him.

We needed a jockey for the Chieftain. Donnie Miller had been the regular jockey for Highland Springs for almost a year, but he had another commitment for the Chieftain, so Barclay and I debated the choice of jockey while Miss Josh warmed up. A bystander, Mitch Berman, who ran the race-replay room at the Maryland tracks and who was an astute observer of the game, piped up.

"Why don't you use this jockey," he said, nodding to the monitor. "He seems to be a good rider."

He was talking about a new jockey to the Maryland tracks, Edgar Prado, who happened to be riding Miss Josh that day.

Miss Josh won again and wasn't claimed. Prado got her to relax and then kicked on to the lead on the turn. She seemed to win with something left. After going winless since December, we had won three races in twelve days in June. We were rolling, and when Barc asked Prado to ride the Springer in the Chieftain, he accepted.

Four days later we were back at the track in full force for the Chieftain Handicap. It had poured the day before and the turf was soft, but the racing secretary kept the race on the grass. Racing fans reflected our confidence at the betting windows by making Highland Springs the third choice at 5-1 behind the overwhelming favorite, Ten Keys. When the gates opened, Prado sent the Springer to an early lead and then eased back to lie third down the backside. Ten Keys sat at the back of the pack on the soft turf. With a half-mile to run, Prado put Highland Springs in gear and took the lead. We were on our feet by then, cheering wildly.

After six furlongs in 1:16 1/5 — on good ground it might have been six seconds faster — Highland Springs felt the whip for the first time in his career on grass. He surged forward but behind him was a whirlwind gathering strength. Ten Keys, who would win $1.2 million in his career, had swung wide around the turn and was picking horses off easily. By the time the field straightened for the drive to the wire, track announcer Trevor Denman could see clearly what was about to take place.

"Highland Springs finds more at the rail, but Ten Keys looks to have his measure ... Ten Keys is going two [strides] to his one ... Ten Keys takes the lead with an eighth of a mile to go."

Still, Highland Springs held on for second in a $60,000 stakes race. While the race was going on, and even years later when I reflected on the outcome, Highland Springs didn't appear good enough to win the race.

"Maybe it was because of the soft turf," I thought but did not say.

"He's still undefeated on firm turf."

We celebrated anyway. Why not? We had bred two stakes horses — though one of them was the bogus Royal Highlander — and it seemed Millsie was continuing to throw a good horse every year. And she hadn't missed a year so far. In a business where one is lucky to average two foals every three years, Millsie had produced six foals in six years, and Tom Hinkle had called earlier to say that she was in foal to the great Spectacular Bid, the second-best runner I ever saw. Millsie was starting to refute every negative thing I ever had said about her.

As quick as a finger snap, the Springer's next race was upon us. We had decided to run him back in the $75,000 Fort McHenry Handicap at Laurel Park on July 3. The race was a mile on the turf, and Edgar Prado stayed on the horse. Ten Keys returned as the favorite.

Eighteen people went to the track with us, including my mother-in-law, down from upstate New York to check on the progress of her daughter. Rita, in her seventh month, was having a wonderful pregnancy and went to the track with the rest of us.

Highland Springs was the third or fourth choice in the *Daily Racing Form* and the *Washington Post*, but the race fans had other ideas. They bet him down to 3-1.

The Springer drew the number nine post position in the eleven-horse field, and that meant he probably would be wide going into the first turn, not a good thing. The turf course at Laurel is one mile, which meant the location of the starting gate was the finish line. The Springer would have a short run into the first turn.

Finally, a few minutes before six, it was post time. Our group had boxes in the grandstand, but filled with nervous energy and tension, we all milled about in the aisle outside the boxes.

The starter tripped the gate, and Highland Springs came out running. Prado asked him for speed right away, took him across the field when clear, and settled on the rail as he went into the turn. He hadn't lost an inch being wide, a nifty piece of race riding. With seven-eighths of a mile to run, some in our group began to cheer. Not me. I liked to watch the early going and kept my mouth shut.

After gunning him from the start, Prado eased Springer off the lead with a gentle hold, letting three horses pass him on the backstretch. The leader edged two lengths away from our boy, and one of the people with us — a race rookie — moaned, "Oh, no! He's lost!"

Ten Keys sat in his customary spot in the back of the pack, but the field was bunched tightly. Six lengths probably separated the leader from the trailer. Prado waited in fourth as the field passed the half-mile pole. That's where he had sent the Springer to the lead in the Chieftain, and he had come up short in the race. Now Prado bided his time, sitting on the rail two lengths from the lead and looking for an opening. The leader was hugging the rail, and with two horses outside him, Prado would need some luck to get through. With three-eighths of a mile to the finish, Prado was still stuck. Then, just like in his first win two years earlier, luck smiled on the Springer. The leader began to tire and slide away from the rail. Prado saw the opening and asked the Springer for acceleration. The gelding immediately shot through the hole and took the lead with about a quarter-mile to run. Right behind him was Kent Desormeaux on Band Leader, a 13-1 shot. As Prado had done with Highland Springs, he also had sat chilly on the rail, waiting for an opening. When he saw the Springer go through, Desormeaux asked his horse and got a response. The pair quickly passed the tiring leader, swung outside, and began their run at Highland Springs. Highland Springs and Band Leader pulled away from the field. Ten Keys started to make a run from the back of the pack, but it clearly wasn't going to be his day.

Yard by yard Band Leader closed on Highland Springs. Trevor Denman was in full voice by then.

"They're coming down to the eighth pole, Highland Springs ... here comes Band Leader on the outside to take him on! These two are going to fight it out ... Highland Springs and Edgar Prado hanging on; Band Leader and Kent Desormeaux closing on the outside!"

Band Leader had the momentum. We all could see that. All I wanted at that moment was for the wire to come up and for the race to be over. Band Leader continued to cut the margin. The noise around me gained intensity. It was the sound of our group cheering.

"Highland Springs and Band Leader going to the wire together …"

Band Leader was close enough to win. Prado had been strapping Highland Springs left-handed, and our gelding was giving his all but was tiring. Desormeaux still was getting a run out of Band Leader. The lead vanished as they passed the wire.

"… At the wire it's close. I think Highland Springs, but it's tight!" Denman called at the finish.

We collapsed into our chairs in the boxes, unsure if we had won. We had the lead to the last instant, but did we have it when it counted? Track officials had not called a winner, official or unofficial. They started to run the replay on the monitors, and they slowed down the tape as the horses ran the last one hundred yards. It was excruciating to watch Band Leader cut the Springer's margin. Finally the horses flashed under the wire, and I could see that the Springer had won by a bare nose. The track usher came to get us to go to the winner's circle; our first stakes win!

There were great cheers when Highland Springs finally was led into the circle. We patted his nose and hugged his neck and smiled for the photo. It was a marvelous moment. All at once it hit me. "Oh my God, he just won $50,000!" I exclaimed.

I was wrong. He had won $51,810. Only five weeks earlier he had been a bad third in the allowance race at Delaware Park. Now he was a stakes winner with about $170,000 in total winnings. We called Sandra Forbush, the first believer in the horse, to tell her the good news.

"I told you that he was going to be a nice horse," she reminded me.

Tom Hinkle called the next morning to congratulate us on the win. I asked him what he thought Highland Mills was worth.

"Do you think she's worth $100,000?" I asked.

"Well," Hinkle drawled, "I think people would be lined up to buy her at that price. I think she's probably worth more like $200,000."

With a stakes winner in the barn, life was more enjoyable. That week I got a call from a staffer at *The Blood-Horse* magazine. She wanted to get all the facts about Highland Springs.

"Whenever someone wins a stakes race for the first time, I call to get the background information," she said.

"You've got a great job," I responded. "You get to talk to happy people all the time."

Now we looked for the next race, and we found one a few weeks later, the Pennsylvania Governor's Cup, a $65,000 stakes at Penn National. Looking at the possible field, we thought the race should be easier than the Fort McHenry, and Barclay was saying Highland Springs was training better than ever.

"Man, we're going to win another $40,000 just like that," I thought after hearing that. But it was not to be. It rained the day before the race, and track officials took the race off the grass, so we scratched our horse. We were disappointed.

Stakes horses have to have options, and we had a backup plan. We had nominated Highland Springs to the Daryl's Joy Stakes, a grade III, $75,000 stakes on opening day at Saratoga. While one door had closed, we had made sure another would open.

Barclay Tagg

Bonner and I celebrate Royal
Mountain Inn's Man o' War victory.

From left to right: My mother, Joyce Rowand; me; four-year-old Michael;
Bonner; Rita; and Bonner's daughter, Kristine Rich. In the back is
Bonner's son, Hudson Young.

**Highland Mills (right) and her daughter, Rejoyced, at Hidaway Farm,
where they were broodmares together.**

Highland Springs winning his first race, a $6,500 maiden claimer at Pimlico in 1987.

Highland Springs winning the 1989 Daryl's Joy Handicap over Fourstardave.

Miss Josh in Australia.

**Miss Josh winning the 1991 Gamely Handicap
at Hollywood Park.**

Highland Crystal winning her first allowance race.

**Highland Crystal winning the 1992 Violet Handicap
at The Meadowlands.**

Royal Mountain Inn as a yearling at Rocketts Mill Farm in Doswell, Virginia, in 1990.

Royal Mountain Inn, with Julie Krone aboard, after winning the 1994 Man o' War Stakes at Belmont Park.

Royal Mountain Inn winning the Man o' War and
Bonner (below) leading him to the winner's circle.

Chapter

*F*or owners and trainers on the East Coast, Saratoga means one thing: the best racing meet in the country. So when we decided to run Highland Springs in a graded stakes race at Saratoga, we knew we were trying to win at what may be the toughest racing venue in America. And, we were trying to win with a gelding two races removed from the claiming ranks. The task was formidable, and I justifiably worried he wouldn't match up to the competition.

The *Racing Form* handicappers weren't crazy about our chances, but one bit of good luck fell our way. So many horses had entered that the racing secretary split the race into two divisions, and we had drawn into the easier group. However, the program had Highland Springs as the longest shot in the field at 12-1.

The other owners in our group flew up on race day. One of them, Eleanor Jones, had taken the day off from her job at IBM, leaving on her office door a sign that said: "Gone to Saratoga." Rita, about a month from delivering our baby, also joined us.

We borrowed Tyson Gilpin's front-row box, and the track gave us a couple more. My in-laws arrived with an entourage from Johnstown, thirty-five miles away. A busload of customers who had heard about our horse from my father-in-law as he tended bar, came to the track that day, intent on betting on Dutch's horse. (Dutch was my German-born father-in-law's nickname.) Meanwhile, countless other customers stayed in Johnstown and bet at the off-track betting parlor there.

The day dragged, with computer problems slowing down the betting machines. Finally, the first half of the Daryl's Joy Stakes was run, and, as I figured, the big favorite, Steinlen, won easily.

After Paul Mellon, who lived in the same Virginia county as I do, won the next race with a two-year-old first-time starter named Red Ransom, who broke an old track record, it was time for us to go to the paddock.

There we found Barclay, fuming.

"They called us to the paddock an hour ago, and they've had us circling a tree for forty-five minutes," he seethed.

Barclay didn't like anything out of place, and he was annoyed at being called to the paddock by someone who hadn't gotten the message that computer glitches had delayed the race. Though Highland Springs had a chance to work himself into a lather in anticipation of a race, he hadn't. He looked like an old cow walking around the paddock, moving calmly and easily.

I checked the odds board. It showed that New York bettors weren't impressed with our boy. He was the longest shot on the board at 14-1. I could understand. After all, the only thing he had won was a small stakes race in Maryland by a diminishing nose margin, carrying 112 pounds, and now he was in the big time. Today he was stepping up in class and carrying 122 pounds. Any normal method of handicapping would predict the Springer getting beaten.

Edgar Prado had come up from his base in Maryland to ride the gelding again, and Barclay gave him instructions and threw him on. The paddock emptied as owners, trainers, and various hangers-on went back to their seats.

Standing in the box as the horses warmed up, my mother-in-law leaned over to speak with Barclay.

"I was there when he won his first stakes race, and I'm here today," she explained in her German-American accent.

"If we win today, the next time he runs we're going to send a limo to pick you up," Barclay replied with a laugh.

The Springer had drawn the number four post position, and he slid into the three hole when a horse inside him was scratched. He broke well when they sent the field away.

Soviet Lad, trained by the venerable Woody Stephens, took the early lead, with Highland Springs tracking him along the hedge. Favored Fourstardave — who would become a Saratoga legend by winning at least one race at Saratoga annually for eight straight years — was to the Springer's outside, and the two horses vied for second down the backstretch. Up in the announcer's booth Marshall Cassidy was making one of his patented hesitating calls. Seconds would go by without Cassidy saying anything. And he kept calling our horse Highland Spring, which was irritating to my ear.

Prado sat quietly on the Springer until the far turn when he cut him loose, and our horse immediately took the lead. All at once it seemed like a rerun of the Fort McHenry Handicap, this time with Fourstardave rallying strongly outside our gelding.

I noticed that my mother — standing next to me — was screaming at the top of her lungs. She wasn't yelling anything intelligible, just screaming like she was on a roller coaster descending from it highest peak. This race, I think, provided some kind of scream therapy for her.

Meanwhile my wife — eight months pregnant — was doing the same thing next to her mother.

My mother-in-law later told us she thought, "My God, she's going to have this baby right here!"

The run to the finish was easier than in the Fort McHenry, despite the tougher race, tougher horses, and heavier weight. This time, Fourstardave never made the kind of threatening run at the Springer that Band Leader had, and our boy won by a half-length. In his final pronouncement before the finish, Cassidy got it right.

"Highland Springs has the lead!" he said, sounding surprised.

My mother turned to Barclay and asked excitedly, "How many stakes races have you won up here?"

"This is the first!" he exclaimed. Then he thought for a second. "Do you realize that this horse has won half his starts?" he said in amazement.

Ah, sweet victory! Sweet, graded stakes victory at Saratoga. What possibly could be better? We high-tailed our way to the trustees' room, where the track provided champagne for everyone. Then we called Sandra Forbush to tell her the news. She was pleased for us.

Harrison Jones had stayed home, but he was eager to hear what happened, so we called him from the room after we had called Sandra.

"Harrison, he won!" I said.

"No joke!" he replied.

"He won $53,000!"

"No joke!"

"He paid thirty dollars to win!"

"No joke!"

That night Eleanor Jones put her winnings inside her motel pillow and slept about as well as an excited lady with money in her pillow could. And up in Johnstown, a vast infusion of cash descended on the town. Pretty much everybody had bet on "Dutch's horse," so there were smiles all over the place. One man had come to the track and bet $2,000 to win on Highland Springs, and when he won, he took home $30,000 in cash. He didn't know what to do. He didn't want to tell his wife that he had bet that much, so he put the money in a suitcase in the trunk of his car.

Now we were in the enviable position of having a graded stakes winner to manage, and managing a good horse leads to bolder dreams, at least in my case.

"You know, Barclay, we might want to consider the Breeders' Cup Mile," I suggested. Barclay agreed readily, both of us knowing that the horse had to take us there. We weren't going unless we thought — not hoped, but really thought — we had a legitimate chance to win. And that meant that he had to pass the next test, the grade III Saratoga Budweiser Breeders' Cup Handicap, in three weeks.

As race day approached, we had to make an adjustment. Edgar Prado had been suspended for a riding infraction so we needed a new rider. We went back to Kent Desormeaux, who was in the process of setting a world record of 598 races won that year. The record still stands.

The feature of the day was the Hopeful Stakes, the first grade I stakes of the year for two-year-olds, and Cot Campbell had the favorite, the undefeated Summer Squall. Our race was the co-feature, and it turned out our box was directly behind that of some of Cot's partners. We chatted all day.

At noon the track handicappers started talking about the day's races, and when they got to ours, they spoke confidently about one horse, and only one horse, Equalize. That horse had won four straight stakes races, three graded, earlier in the year, and some surmised he was the best turf horse in America.

I was glad that Steinlen wasn't in the field. He had run two-fifths of a second faster on the same course the same day as Highland Springs in his division of the Daryl's Joy. Steinlen's trainer, D. Wayne Lukas, had Slew City Slew in the race, making his first start on the turf. As Lukas watched some horses working that morning, he was questioned about his chances. Lukas said that he thought his colt would run well but then added a warning: "Look out for Tagg's horse. It looks like he can run a bit." Word passes quickly at the racetrack, and that comment got back to us before the race. It gave us all some extra confidence.

Barclay brought the Springer to the paddock; the trainer's mood was much better than it had been before the big horse's previous race.

"I galloped him up here the morning of the last race, and he just went around the track, nothing special," Barclay said. "But this morning he was pulling me around out there. He is ready!"

At 5:10 on that pretty afternoon, the starter sent the field away. Triteamtri took the early lead and set quick fractions on a turf course torn up after four weeks of constant use. Kent settled the Springer into fourth, though never too far back. Equalize, under Angel Cordero, ran fifth early.

Meanwhile, Cassidy was having fun drawing out the names of some of the horses.

"It's Triteamtri on the lead, Sleeew City Sleeew is second … and Mace-o is at the back of the pack," he intoned.

The field hit three-quarters of a mile in 1:09 1/5, sprinting time, and the horses still had more than a quarter-mile to go. Kent had allowed Equalize to pass him on the turn and raced next to last with three furlongs to go, ahead of only Maceo. Around the turn Cordero cut Equalize loose to go after the leaders. Kent quickly made his move with Highland Springs, bringing him to the outside of Equalize. The two horses were now head and head. Cordero drew his stick, but the Springer had the momentum, and he eased past Equalize and took the lead with an eighth of a mile to go. He pulled away from Slew City Slew. Only Maceo was still making up ground.

They passed a mile in 1:32 3/5, but Maceo continued to close. Kent allowed him to go inside Highland Springs in the final yards and watched as Maceo advanced on his left. Maceo got to within a neck … and then the wire flashed, and the race was over. From our position in a box past the finish line, it appeared that Maceo had taken the lead before the wire, and my brother-in-law sat right down on the box steps in disappointment. Meanwhile, I had watched the stretch run on the monitor, and I could see we had won. I told him so, but he didn't move.

"I'm telling you we won!" I shouted. "I'm going to the winner's circle!"

Emotions were running high as our hopes were confirmed. Highland Springs had just set a course record at the cathedral of racing, a mile and a sixteenth in 1:39 1/5. I hurried down the stairs toward the winner's circle.

It was a mob scene. We had a group of about forty — family, friends, and co-owners — there, and the photographer had to take us farther and farther out onto the track to get everybody in the picture. Waiting for the photo, holding up a huge red Budweiser blanket with others in our group, I stood next to Kent, who was speaking quietly to himself.

"You know how long that track record has been there?" he asked rhetorically. "One hundred years! That's how long it's been there. And we just broke it!"

Actually, the record had stood for a little more than nineteen years, but Kent was pumped up and carried away.

We descended on the trustees' room, but then we remembered that the Hopeful still was to be run. We wanted to see Dogwood Stable's Summer Squall, so some of us went back to the box. We were glad we did. In a memorable performance the little son of Storm Bird found himself blocked behind a wall of horses in the stretch. Jockey Pat Day needed a break, and finally, with about an eighth of a mile to run, it came. A tiny sliver showed up between two of the horses, and Summer Squall was into, and then through, it in an instant. Then he ran away from the field, winning impressively. We applauded our friend's horse.

Another jockey claimed foul, and Cot and his partners had to sit through minutes of agony as the stewards reviewed the film before the result was made official. Then all of us went to the trustees' room, and we had one of the most pleasant afternoons I ever experienced in the game.

First they showed our race on the TV monitors, and Cot's group applauded us; next they showed the Hopeful, and our group applauded them. I looked out on a group of fifty or so people, all happy at the same instant and in the same place, and thought, "It isn't often that you get this many happy people together in the same room. We'd better enjoy it."

That afternoon the words on the lips of everybody in that room were the same: "Breeders' Cup."

"I'll see you at the Breeders' Cup," I told Cot, and he said, "Yep, we'll meet again in Florida."

Campaigning Highland Springs was the highlight of my professional career to that point. Winning two graded stakes races at Saratoga, while setting a track record in one, just three months after failing dismally in a tiny allowance race in Delaware, was akin to scaling Mt. Everest after unsuccessfully attempting Mt. Rainier. Two years earlier Highland Springs had won his first race at the absolute bottom of the barrel in Maryland. Now he was one race away from a start in the grade I, million-dollar Breeders' Cup Mile, where he would face the world's best turf milers.

Friends in the horse world told me at the time that I should enjoy what was taking place, that it was a "once in a lifetime" experience. Yet, oddly enough, I didn't think it was. I thought we had other good horses in our hands. We just had to wait.

Most good horses shine from the very beginning. Highland Springs did not. If we had taken him to New York two years earlier and made him run against the quality of horses he had just beaten at Saratoga, he would have been creamed. Of that I am certain. Barclay and his staff had spent a massive amount of time with him, and now it was paying off. It had taken us nine years in the business to get a horse that won $100,000. Highland Springs had won almost $150,000 in twenty-four days, and that drew notice from a variety of corners.

Jennie Rees, the racing reporter for the Louisville *Courier-Journal*, called for an interview and said — and then wrote — that no other horse at the Saratoga meeting had distinguished himself more than Highland Springs.

He had gone north an unknown five-year-old gelding, three races removed from a future of claiming races and oblivion. In twenty-four days he had become a force. I was so proud of what he had accomplished, but more than anything else I wanted him to complete the story. How good a story would it be if this former claimer, this undistinguished gelding by a $3,500 stallion and out of a mare that had won $450 at the races, won the Breeders' Cup Mile? It would be a story of heroic proportions.

While we were winning races and preparing for the 1989 Breeders' Cup, something else demanded my attention. Rita's due date was nearing. She had skipped the second Saratoga stakes race since she was so close to delivery that we were certain they wouldn't let her on a plane. The day after the Labor Day holiday, she went into labor, and that evening she gave birth to a boy. We named him Michael Barclay, and after I called the next morning and left the message on Barc's machine, he called back to say how flattered he was.

Michael Barclay was healthy in all other respects except for a heart murmur. The doctors thought he might have a pulmonary stenosis, a pinch in the artery leading from the heart. They said they might eventually have to fix it.

Mother and baby were doing fine, though, so I felt I could turn my attention back to our racing enterprise.

While the Springer was off making a name for himself, Miss Josh was battling a series of minor infirmities — most often in her feet — that kept her from the races for almost two months. When she did return in early August, we entered her in an allowance race on the grass at Laurel. With Highland Springs' success on that surface, we thought she might do well, in spite of the fact she really wasn't built to be a turf horse. She was put together more like a sprinter and had sufficient early speed to run short distances. But there was something else at play in our decision. The dirt is generally a hard, fast surface. We thought the turf might be kinder on her feet. To a certain extent, we were right. She ran a good second in her first turf race, beaten less than two lengths going a mile, and then her hoof maladies flared up again, and she was on the shelf another two months.

We chose the grade III Kelso Handicap at Belmont Park, four weeks from the Breeders' Cup Mile, for the Springer's last prep race. By then it was clear to me that Steinlen was the horse to beat in the Mile. He had won the grade I Bernard Baruch Handicap at a mile and an eighth at Saratoga and the grade I Arlington Million at a mile and a quarter at Arlington Park. I was hoping Steinlen would go in the Breeders' Cup Turf race, at a mile and a half, but I was preparing for him to be our main competition in the Mile. My calculations said that Highland Springs was one length slower than Steinlen at a mile, and if I was correct, we had a very good chance of winning. While one length may seem almost insignificant over the distance of a mile, it actually represents a significant disparity at the upper levels of the sport. At the time, I thought that if he were one length slower than Steinlen, Highland Springs would be second in the Mile, still a terrific achievement for him.

Before I would commit to running in the Breeders' Cup, I wanted some outside confirmation of how good the Springer was. I called noted racing writer Andy Beyer at his home. "Andy, you don't know me, but I've got a horse named Highland Springs … "

"You've got a very good horse named Highland Springs," Beyer quickly cut in. I was feeling good already.

I told him we were considering running in the Breeders' Cup Mile, and he said he thought we had a chance though we would be a longshot. He agreed that Steinlen was the American horse to beat, and — being an optimistic owner, after all — I hung up feeling like the Mile was within our reach.

Highland Springs trained very well coming into the Kelso Handicap. On a beautiful October day at Belmont Park, with a large crowd of owners in attendance, Highland Springs ran wide around the one big turn in the one-mile stakes race, took the lead with a quarter-mile to go on a course that was not firm, and then tried to hold off the closers. I had expected him to win easily, but he faded just a touch in the lane and was beaten three-quarters of a length for everything.

Four other horses were in that margin, and the air went out of our Breeders' Cup balloon right there at the track. We were stunned with the finish and struggled to understand why he had been off the board for the first time in his grass career, though he was beaten only three parts of a length.

I polled the owners right then about whether they still wanted to go to the Breeders' Cup, and they did. Next I asked Barclay, and he hesitated before replying.

"I still think we should go," he said.

We decided to go on to the Breeders' Cup, but we were going with a lot less optimism than we had displayed five minutes before the Kelso.

That same afternoon Miss Josh returned to the races at Pimlico in a six-furlong allowance race on the dirt. While she won in the very slow time of 1:14, her victory still was a bright spot on the day.

Chapter  18

*"Ah, but a man's reach should exceed his grasp,
or what's a heaven for?"*
Robert Browning

The Breeders' Cup was the brainchild of a number of Kentucky professionals who decided there should be a day of championship racing at the end of the year, and that the minimum purse for each race in the series should be one million dollars. To be eligible for the championship day, as well as for a number of other stakes races with extra money from the Breeders' Cup, the horse needed two things: it needed to be by a nominated stallion, which wasn't hard, as most stallions in America were nominated; and when the horse was a weanling, it needed to be nominated for a five-hundred dollar fee. We always nominated every horse we bred, and Highland Springs already had reaped an additional $60,000 for his win in the Saratoga Breeders' Cup Handicap. To me, it was, and remains, the best five hundred dollars one can spend in racing. Now, if Highland Springs were to win the Mile, we would win almost $500,000 in one race.

In 1989 the Breeders' Cup was run at Gulfstream Park in south Florida for the first time. Looking at that track's configuration, I thought that the Springer would like the smaller turf course, similar to others he had done well on, and the firm surface. All we needed, I thought, was a decent post position. With fourteen horses going into the first turn, an outside post position likely would kill our chances.

We all went to Florida on the Tuesday night before the Breeders' Cup, including eight-week-old Michael Barclay, who handled the flight like a pro. We wanted to be there for the post position draw on Wednesday morning.

I was convinced we had to draw a decent post to have any chance, and never in my life in the horse business had I been so nervous as that morning. When they called Highland Springs' name and then said, "Post position five," I embraced my wife and mother. We had a chance! Especially when Steinlen drew inside us. That meant that Kent Desormeaux could keep a good eye on the horse we thought was the one to beat.

Breeders' Cup horses from all over filled Gulfstream's stables. It was exciting to be in the same company as the champions from America and Europe. As for our race, the pundits were focusing on the unbeaten European Horse of the Year, Zilzal, owned by Sheikh Mana al Maktoum from Dubai. I had followed Zilzal's career, and I was sure he would not be a contender. The reports from Europe said he sweated up before his races. I thought, "If he's sweating up in Europe, what's he going to do when he hits the south Florida heat and humidity, especially with a winter coat growing?"

No, to me the one to beat was Steinlen, owned by Paris art dealer Daniel Wildenstein, and since I also was convinced our horse was within one length of that horse, the worst we could do if we ran our race, was to finish second, maybe third. That would still be a triumph to me. And, besides, suppose Steinlen had a bad day? Maybe we could find a way to make up that one length.

Imagine my surprise when I opened the *Racing Form* and actually looked at the records of the entries other than Steinlen. I went down horse after horse, and I was having trouble throwing any of them out. That's when a great truth dawned on me: We might be within a length of the best horse in the field, but there were a handful of other horses in the same spot. For the first time I understood that the increments separating one horse from another at that level are so small as to be microscopic. If the race were run ten times, we would win once, maybe twice, if we got really lucky, but no more than that. Of course, you could say the same thing about most of the rest, but that was no solace.

Breeders' Cup excitement builds in the two days leading up to the races.

Nobody has lost at that point. The atmosphere becomes more and more electric. Thursday morning Highland Springs was due to have his last workout on the turf course. We all were there to see him jog clockwise around the course and pull to a stop right in front of us. He was wearing a purple Breeders' Cup saddle cloth with his name on it. Then, when the moment was right, the rider asked him, and he took off. To me, he didn't seem to be running that fast. With my binoculars I watched him all the way to the finish and then picked up the phone in the stand that connects to the people who actually timed the works.

"How fast did you get Highland Springs?" I asked.

"Well, we couldn't time him for the three-eighths work, but he got the last quarter [mile] in a sensational twenty-three seconds flat."

I hung up. Did he say "sensational"? I scurried over to the gap in the hedge where the horses came off the track. I met Barclay as he picked up the horse and rider, David Carroll, who was the regular exercise rider for Easy Goer — the favorite for the Breeders' Cup Classic — and who now is a successful trainer in his own right.

"Man, if he runs like that on Saturday, they're going to pay you a lot of money," Carroll gushed.

My head was spinning. A "sensational" work? "Pay me a lot of money?" These were neutral parties. They had no association with the horse or us, and they were really pumping up our chances. That night at the media party things got even better. A reporter I had met came to me to ask if I knew how fast Highland Springs had worked.

"Sure," I said. "Twenty-three flat."

"No," he corrected. "He worked in :22 3/5. It was the best workout of any of the turf horses down here. The clocker said he's going to bet on him if the turf is firm."

It was hard to sleep that night.

After the workout Highland Springs seemed to thrive. The next day, Friday, twenty-four hours from the race, he looked a picture of health grazing in the afternoon. The sun glinted off his coat. He was as good as hands could make him.

"Barc, he's perfect," I said. "You've done a magnificent job getting him here. Now let's just hope for some racing luck."

Race day dawned bright and warm with a trace of clouds, and I was up early and ready to go as soon as I could get everybody else moving. On the way to the track, I saw dark clouds, and by the time we arrived and walked to the entrance, it started to pour. We ducked under a cover and waited for it to stop. Standing there, holding my son, I let my emotions get the better of me. I started to cry. I just couldn't understand how we could have come so far and done so much to be denied a fair chance when it mattered most. I knew that on a soft turf course the Springer wouldn't have a chance to run his best, and that's all I wanted: a chance to see how he would do against the best in the world.

The downpour over, I wasn't certain if I even wanted to run and debated the idea with the other owners. They left it in my hands. I called the barn and left a message that Barclay could scratch the horse if he wanted. In the era before cell phones, Barc had no way of contacting me, but he didn't scratch Highland Springs. The horse was coming into the race so well, he wanted to take his chances. The course was rated "good" for the Mile, and I thought that helped the European horses the most, but still, to me, the one to beat didn't change: Steinlen, who, by the way, had raced in Europe at the beginning of his career.

The excitement of the moment gone for me, the day seemed endless. Finally, it was time for us to go to the paddock, and the air was warm and sticky by then. Kent Desormeaux came bounding into the paddock, a picture of a teenager ready to make something happen. It was his first Breeders' Cup runner. With eleven minutes to go, Barclay pitched him aboard the Springer, and we went back to our seats, ready to watch whatever might happen. I checked the odds board. Highland Springs was 35-1, a longshot but at least not the longest shot, with five horses at higher odds. Zilzal was favored, with Steinlen the second choice.

Michael Barclay had been napping on and off throughout the day, and he chose that time to take another one. We laid him sideways on one of the chairs and prepared to watch the race.

One thing I could clearly see was that the favorite was a mess. Sweat dripped off him, and he didn't want to go onto the turf course. He looked terrible, and a couple of others didn't warm up too well. Finally, it was race time.

Highland Springs came out running. Kent got him away quickly and took an ideal position in the run into the first turn. He was one length behind the speed horses, Quick Call and Simply Majestic, and just outside Steinlen. We couldn't have drawn it up any better. Meanwhile, Zilzal — who was used to having the lead — got off a step slowly and was back in the pack and wide.

As the field moved into the turn, Desormeaux tightened things up on Steinlen, pushing him perilously close to the hedge. Steinlen's jockey, Jose Santos, pushed back, so these two "layed [sic] on each other in the run to the first turn," as the *Racing Form* chart caller wrote. The pace wasn't fast for these kinds of horses, a testimony to the course condition.

When they straightened for a run up the backstretch, Simply Majestic took the lead and edged away under Angel Cordero. Quick Call was second, and then Kent decided to slip inside the longshot Green Line Express and take third. Steinlen, meanwhile, was on the hedge with horses in front and beside him.

Down on the track apron, Steinlen's trainer, D. Wayne Lukas, could see his worst fears materializing. Followed by a TV camera person, Lukas had his conversation recorded.

"He's pinned back," he said flatly to an assistant. "He can't get through."

"They've got him trapped," the assistant said.

"Yep … he's not going to get through," Lukas said.

At the quarter pole Kent asked Highland Springs for speed, and our boy responded.

"Simply Majestic comes roaring off the turn," announcer Tom Durkin called. "Highland Springs attacks on the outside!"

Barclay said later that that was the moment when he thought the race was ours. Highland Springs was moving well. He had momentum, and Kent whapped him twice on the right side, switched his stick to his left hand and hit him twice again. Highland Springs cut the margin. He was a half-length from the lead.

Up in the stands, the noise level in our area increased tenfold. My mother looked at the sleeping Michael and noted that, while he didn't wake up, he started sucking his pacifier much faster.

Turning for home, Steinlen had extricated himself from the trap, but he still had horses everywhere around him. He needed luck, and the jock needed skill to bring him home first.

Kent was a hurricane of energy, asking for more run and getting it from the Springer. We were close enough to the leader that if Simply Majestic had been a birthday cake, Highland Springs could have blown out the candles. They were an eighth of a mile from the wire and the race was there for anybody to take. Kent went to switch his stick back to his right hand … and it flew out into space and fell between the legs of the rallying Sabona. Kent seemed stunned for a second, but then he applied all the skill and force he had, pushing, pushing, pushing the Springer. He kept coming.

Meanwhile, Jose Santos decided to make his own luck. He cut to the hedge right in front of the tiring Quick Call, causing jockey Pat Day to rein in the spent competitor. Now he had his racing room, and when Santos asked for a response, he got it.

For a second, Steinlen, Simply Majestic, and Highland Springs were nose to nose for the lead. But Steinlen had the finishing kick and went on. Seeing that he wasn't going to get past Simply Majestic, let alone Steinlen, Kent eased off and let the Springer finish on his own. Four horses passed him in the final thirty yards.

Highland Springs ran seventh, beaten a little more than two lengths for everything.

I think it unlikely we could have won that day, not on the softer turf and not with the jockey dropping the stick, but I would have liked to find out for sure. You see, Highland Springs never got another chance to show that he belonged with the best in the world. He never ran in another Breeders' Cup. This was it, and all the chart shows is that a 35-1 shot ran seventh in the 1989 Breeders' Cup Mile. On the surface, it seems about where a longshot should run.

He may not have been good enough to win, even with a perfect trip and a firm turf course. I just wish he had been able to run his race, fair and square, and then, win or lose, I could have accepted the outcome. As it is, it nags at me to this day. I guess the Mile experience shows that — no matter how much we desire them — some things are not meant to be.

Kent moved on to ride in California, and I think he may have ridden for us once after the Breeders' Cup. In 2003, however, I ran into him at the media party for the Breeders' Cup at Santa Anita. Michael Barclay, age fourteen at the time, was getting photos and autographs of jockeys, and when I saw Kent, I took my son over to him. Desormeaux was talking to someone else at the time, and we waited patiently. Then he turned my way and pointed straight at me like he recognized me.

"Kent, you don't remember me, but …," I started.

"Oh, yes, I do," he responded quickly. "I rode your horse in the Breeders' Cup. I dropped the stick at the eighth pole. I apologize."

I was stunned he had remembered.

"Yeah, well … I know that you were doing your best to win."

He looked me right in the eye before saying, "I promise you, I would have given my life to win that race for you."

"And besides, we wouldn't even have gotten to the Breeders' Cup if you hadn't ridden so well in that race at Saratoga," I said.

"We ran a mile in 1:32 3/5," he said. "I remember it like it was yesterday."

We took photos, and he hugged Michael, and then we went off and I started to calculate how remarkable it was that Kent remembered so much. The race had been fourteen years earlier. Riding more than a thousand horses a year, Kent could have ridden about twenty thousand horses since he sat on Highland Springs, and still he remembered details about a horse that he had ridden to one stakes victory. Amazing.

Chapter 19

The 1980s closed with a fabulous year for us. Highland Springs began 1989 struggling to win low-level allowance races and ended it as a multiple graded stakes winner, probably one of the top-fifteen turf horses in the country. It was all good, and as with anybody who has ever had a good run at something, we thought it would last forever.

After the Breeders' Cup, Highland Springs ran only four more races. He finished a disappointing third — as the 6-5 favorite — in a grade III stakes seven weeks after the Breeders' Cup, then won the grade III Appleton Handicap at one mile at Gulfstream Park on January 21, 1990. He ran the distance two seconds faster than Steinlen had on Breeders' Cup day, an indication, I think, of how soft the turf actually had been on Breeder's Cup day. About a month later he finished a close third in the mile and a sixteenth Fort Lauderdale Handicap, and on March 10 he finished a bad fourth in the grade III Gulfstream Park Budweiser Breeders' Cup. Barclay had been struggling to keep Highland Springs' ankles in racing shape throughout the gelding's career, but, finally, they gave out.

We gave him time off, hoping to bring him back, but he never ran another race. Still, he had amassed more than $400,000 in earnings, and he did far more than simply earn money for us.

When Highland Springs came along, I was at the lowest point in my professional career. He picked me up, gave me the enthusiasm and the means to go on, and saved my dream. He proved to me I didn't go completely wrong by giving up my law career to pursue something so difficult. Highland Springs did as much for me as a horse could ever do for a person, and I was grateful beyond words.

We returned Highland Springs to Foxhall Farm, back to Sandra Forbush, the person who had believed in him first and longest. He went back into the same paddocks he had run in as a yearling. I went to visit one day, and we saddled him up, and I got on him. Then I really understood what jockeys had meant when they would say: "He's a push-button horse." When I was on him, I found he would do whatever you asked, whenever you wanted.

Miss Josh had gone to Florida with Highland Springs in the winter of 1990. After winning an allowance race in October 1989, she had gone downhill. She was beaten almost twenty lengths in a six-furlong allowance race on the dirt three weeks later, and then, three weeks after that, she was fourth in a mile and a sixteenth allowance race.

Her feet were problematic. X-rays that winter showed chips in her ankles — which, miraculously, never bothered her — and that her coffin bones were rotated downward, which meant they tended to make the bottom of her hooves sore. By great day-to-day efforts Barclay and his staff were able to keep her going, and she was a good-feeling kind of horse, in spite of her hoof maladies. Training at Gulfstream Park, Barc had her ready for an allowance race in early February.

Ridden by Jean Cruguet, who had ridden Seattle Slew to victory in the 1977 Triple Crown, Joshie faced a strong allowance field — including the likes of Personal Business, who would become a grade I stakes winner that year at Saratoga — and she simply demolished them. Cruguet sent her right to the lead in the seven-furlong dirt race and pushed her to keep going. She opened up a couple of lengths on the field after a quarter-mile and kept pulling away. She won by six and a quarter lengths.

Though she had never won on the grass, we kept trying her on that surface. She had a sprinter's pedigree and body, but oftentimes horses like that can run farther on the generally kinder grass surfaces. After the win at Gulfstream, we tried her back on the turf, and she was a sharp third against stakes horses. Speaking with Barclay after the race, I noted a hint of admiration in his voice for the first time.

"This is no bad filly now," he said. "No bad filly."

I had always liked Miss Josh. It's sometimes hard to understand why some people fall in love with certain horses, but this one was easy. Miss Josh was a classic bay horse — mahogany with a black mane and tail, and black points from the knee down — and she had a pretty head and a beautiful eye. There was not a speck of white on her, and she had a very sweet nature … toward humans. Toward other horses, she exhibited a toughness and a competitiveness I hadn't seen in one of our horses since Fragile Dream had been in training. Those were the qualities that endeared her to me, well after I had been taken in by her looks.

After her good race on the grass in Florida, Barclay started her on the dirt, with predictable results. She was fifth, beaten by more than eighteen lengths. Barclay shipped her to Maryland and gave her two months off to help her recover. She reappeared in a $50,000 claimer going six furlongs on the dirt at Pimlico. We were taking a chance, but with those feet we didn't think any trainer would take her, even though she might have residual value as a broodmare prospect. As the half sister to Highland Springs and the stakes-placed Royal Highlander, she had a pedigree that might look good on a sales catalog page one day. Still we were willing to take the small chance she would get claimed to give her the opportunity of running and winning against cheaper horses.

Miss Josh broke slowly in the field that day and lagged early. On the turn, jockey Marco Castaneda sent her after the leaders, and announcer Trevor Denman called out, "Miss Josh is making her run from the back of the pack."

They straightened out for the run down the stretch, and Denman's South African accent and phrasing resonated throughout the stands.

"Miss Josh is beginning to roll on the grandstand side … here comes Miss Josh like an express train down the center of the course! … If you've got your money on Miss Josh, you can head to the windows and be first in line, she's won it easy!"

Seven months earlier she had won at the same distance and at the same racetrack. That day it took her 1:14, and the jockey hit her fourteen times in the stretch. Now, she won in 1:10 3/5, and she was under a hand ride most of the way. It was clear she had improved significantly, a fact that hadn't gone unnoticed among other trainers. Back in the video room, watching all views of the race, sat another trainer. "If this filly were in New York, trainers would be knocking over gas stations to get the money to claim her," he said.

We all laughed, but the obvious threat in his opinion opened my eyes. I had the impression he might have wanted to claim her himself but had talked himself out of it at the last moment. We decided that was her last claiming race, at least for so long as she could compete in allowance races.

We tried her on the grass again three weeks later in allowance company, and she killed the field, going a mile and a sixteenth. Lying just off a quick pace, she won as rider Marco Castaneda pleased, with Trevor Denman calling out, "Miss Josh is drawing off impressively under a hand ride to win this one well."

I thought Miss Josh might be like Highland Springs in that she might be able to string together her good races. She had won two in a row and dominated her previous start. It was time for a stakes race.

We sought an easy spot and thought we had found one in the Penn National Budweiser Breeders' Cup Handicap, a $75,000 stakes at a mile and a sixteenth on the grass. We entered her and drove three hours to the track in Grantville, Pennsylvania. A group of our owners also made the trip in a van, the passengers pouring mixed drinks for the occasion. Along the way I stopped and called Penn National and heard the news that the high-weight and presumed favorite, Fieldy, had been scratched from the race. When we caught up to the van and told everyone the news, they started honking the horn and applauding. As Forrest Gump might have said, "That's good. One less thing."

Miss Josh looked terrific in the paddock, wiggling with energy while they tried to saddle her. Jockey Mario Pino — who had never ridden for us — came up in our silks. I had my serious game face on when we were introduced in the paddock. There was no joking around. I was all business, and before he was thrown on her, I had a forecast for him.

"Don't worry about anything," I said. "When this filly changes leads in the stretch, she'll blow the doors off these other fillies."

He looked at me like I had ridden to the track in the van with the drinkers.

It turned out I was right. Miss Josh sat close to the early pace, went to the lead on the turn, and sprinted away from the others when she changed leads. She won by three marvelous lengths. We sped down the stairs to get to the track apron and then to the winner's circle. All the way I kept saying, "Two stakes winners! Millsie has produced two stakes winners!"

In the winner's circle after the race, I shook hands with Pino. He had some wonder in his voice when he said, "She did it just like you said she would. When she changed leads in the stretch, boom, she was gone!"

Miss Josh surpassed $115,000 in earnings with her victory, and we thought that given the way she had run in Pennsylvania, bigger days awaited her. We decided to wheel her right back in seventeen days and run her in the grade II Matchmaker Stakes at Atlantic City Race Course.

The Matchmaker was a unique stakes in that the first three finishers won breeding seasons to selected stallions the following year in addition to the winner's share of the $150,000 purse. The race had a storied past, and we were hoping she would add her name to the list of famous winners. It was not to be. When the gates opened, she took the early lead, and after the first quarter mile I knew we were finished. I looked on in dismay as Pino had her clipping along, and I knew the outcome. There was no way she was going to lead that field from gate to wire, not going a mile and three-sixteenths. It wasn't that she was going so fast. I honestly cannot recall the early fractions. It's just that she wasn't bred to get that distance in the first place, and if she ever did, it would be because she was the best horse in the field. With a nice mare like Capades in this

Matchmaker, Joshie would need to be ridden conservatively, cautiously, warily. She would have to sneak up on the opposition and pounce when her competitors weren't expecting it. Had she been able to step up and win the Matchmaker, it would have opened up the world to her, but standing there, watching her go down the backside on the lead, I could see that wasn't going to happen.

She petered out on the turn for home, having already run a mile, and sauntered in sixth, beaten more than seven lengths. No one noticed her. She was just another filly that seemed in over her head. We regrouped. We ran her back next at Pimlico in the Sensational Handicap, a $60,000 stakes at a mile and a sixteenth, and she won by a length and a half, though she was not impressive. She had slowed down in the stretch once she had taken the lead, and the jock had to push her to the wire. Still, she was a multiple stakes winner of more than $150,000, giving her dam, Highland Mills, a more impressive produce record, especially considering that the sires of Highland Springs and Miss Josh together cost us a paltry total of $10,000 in stud fees.

We all trooped into the winner's circle, including my father. My dad was an engineer, and he never was interested in sports of any kind. Mother was the one who thought they should buy into the horses, and my dad showed little interest in what was going on, especially in the early, losing years. (He did, however, find the activity in the breeding shed at Gainesway Farm one Sunday afternoon very interesting … the screaming stallion, the compliant mare with the leather coat on her neck and back for protection from the stallion's bites. Mother — a properly brought up Southern lady — had stayed outside while a mare was bred to Riverman, but then her curiosity got the better of her and she bugged my sister to tell her everything that had transpired.)

When our racing luck finally turned around, my father seemed puzzled and then amazed. He never said anything, but I saw him looking at our horses winning races and could see the wheels turning in his brain. "How can this be happening?" I imagined him thinking. He just couldn't seem to believe we could breed a horse and then have it win the way Highland Springs and, now, Miss Josh had. A ham radio operator his whole life, he would get on his set every week and talk with his buddies around the country, and the prime focus of his conversations became the horses. It was astonishing to him.

While Bonner Farm was focused on Miss Josh at the moment, that wasn't all that was happening. Highland Mills' next foal in line, Ferebee, a three-year-old filly, was a cheap claimer who won for us and was claimed by horseman Russell Jones. We had Millsie's two-year-old filly by Raise a Man, named Highland Crystal, and a yearling colt by Vigors who was called Royal Mountain Inn after the restaurant owned by my in-laws. Highland Crystal wasn't nearly as attractive as Miss Josh. A bay filly with some white on her, she had a plain face, a long nose, and a small body. When Miss Josh picked her head up and stared into the distance, she looked regal. There was nothing regal about Highland Crystal, but Sandra Forbush's farm manager liked the filly. What was more encouraging was that Sandra liked the Vigors colt. He was going to be the biggest horse out of Highland Mills, and though The Jockey Club papers called his coat roan — red hairs mixed with white — he clearly was going to turn gray.

"He's so light on his feet for a big horse," Sandra would say. "You should see him run in the paddocks … It's like he doesn't touch the ground at all."

It was about this time that I stepped back to consider where Bonner Farm was headed. After six awful years we were rolling, with two straight stakes winners. Now the partners were making money, and everybody was having a good time. If there ever were a time to expand, bring in new partners, and buy more horses, it was then, but that didn't interest me. It occurred to me I really didn't enjoy the business part of Bonner Farm too much. What I liked most was planning the breeding of the mares and managing the racing careers of the horses. Driving me was the thought that it had taken a decade to get to the point where I had some good horses to manage, and I was going to apply all my energies to making sure they succeeded. Miss Josh was a good filly. I wanted to see if I could help her become better.

little less than three weeks after the Sensational Handicap win, we sent Miss Josh back to Atlantic City to run in the Atlantic City Budweiser Breeders' Cup Handicap, a $150,000 race at a mile and a sixteenth on the grass. It attracted a much easier field than the Matchmaker, but on race day it rained extraordinarily hard. Every time I called the racing secretary's office on the way to the track, the staff assured me the race would be run on the grass, no matter what.

Many of the other top turf contenders scratched, so the race would be easy money, if Miss Josh could handle soft turf, but like Highland Springs before her, she couldn't. The second choice, she spun her wheels all the way around and was beaten by fourteen lengths. Nevertheless, her efforts were good enough for third place. I wasn't discouraged. She came out of the race well; she won almost $18,000; and we learned she couldn't run her best on soft turf. We sent her out seventeen days later in the Violet Handicap, a grade III stakes at The Meadowlands.

We had never run a horse at The Meadowlands, just across the Hudson River from New York City. Like the Atlantic City races, the race was at night, and The Meadowlands invited all the owners of horses in the stakes race to dinner in the Pegasus Room at the top of the track. Looking out on a clear, fall evening, we could see the New York City skyline.

Miss Josh seemed to have adapted well to the different routine — a van ride at an odd hour, running under the lights, and a change in her feeding and sleeping schedule — and she came to the paddock on her toes. Seeing that, I felt confident and excited. I thought her last race was a throw-out. She simply hadn't liked the soft turf, but this course was firm.

The Violet drew a field of fourteen, reduced to thirteen when morning-line favorite Paris Opera scratched. Looking at the program, I could see we had stepped up significantly in class. The list of owners told me that. The favorite, Invited Guest — owned by prominent businessman R.D. Hubbard — was a graded stakes winner from California. Centennial Farms had grade II winner Topicount. Diana Firestone had Gather the Clan, the Violet winner the year before. Then there was Summer Secretary. Trained by Allen Jerkens — known as the Giant Killer for his uncanny ability to send out lesser horses to upset the likes of Secretariat — five-year-old Summer Secretary had won about $500,000. I didn't know which opponent to fear most.

Joshie came out of the gate well, and Summer Secretary, under Jacinto Vasquez, took the early lead. Mario Pino settled Joshie into fourth, two lengths back as they straightened out for the run down the backstretch. The early pace was comfortable.

As the racing manager, I would examine each of our horses' races over and over. How fast had they run each quarter-mile? When they ran well, where were they in the body of the race? And — at least as important — what factors had gone into a poor showing? I already knew Miss Josh could not win a good race on the lead, and time after time I saw something else: Miss Josh ran best when she could run her first half-mile in about forty-eight seconds. Faster than that, and she came up empty.

Focusing on the action on the backstretch, I saw Miss Josh about three lengths behind Summer Secretary as announcer Dave Johnson called out, "Summer Secretary has the lead after a half in :47 1/5." Good.

Mario Pino had succeeded in getting Joshie to relax, but as the field entered the second turn, he let out the reins a bit and the result was instantaneous. She flew past three other horses and took dead aim on the leader. Dave Johnson took notice.

"Summer Secretary has the lead … Miss Josh, with a big move on the outside, now up to challenge the leader!"

As Miss Josh easily cruised to the flank of Summer Secretary, she expected that horse to crumble. Summer Secretary didn't. A horse doesn't win a half-million dollars without having some determination, and when

Joshie rolled to her, Summer Secretary accelerated. She wasn't about to give up the lead so easily. The two pulled away from the other horses.

Miss Josh took a brief lead, but Summer Secretary came right back at her. Depending on the stride, they exchanged the lead back and forth. Dave Johnson seemed so caught up in the drama playing itself out below him that he almost forgot his trademark phrase … but not quite.

"They're noses apart, and down the stretch they come! Miss Josh on the outside, Summer Secretary on the rail!"

Pino turned his stick up and popped Miss Josh once. She flipped her tail and dug in one more time.

"Miss Josh by half a length!" Johnson called as the two hit the wire.

We flew to the winner's circle. My wife wasn't there; she was home with Michael. My sister wasn't there; she was in Kentucky for the Keeneland sale. But a lot of our other partners had come to watch, and I was beaming. With that victory Joshie was a graded stakes winner. Talking with trainer John Forbes afterwards — he was a friend of my Aunt Bunky — I confidently replied to his question about where I would take Joshie next.

"We're going to the All Along," I said.

The All Along Stakes was a $300,000, grade II stakes at Laurel Park. Finally Joshie could run in a decent stakes at her home track. As a long-time racing fan, I had attended the Washington, D.C., International festival of races, which brings together the best turf runners in the world, for a decade and a half. I had taken novice race fans there with me. Now I was going to be competing as an owner, and I was very excited.

I respected the All Along Stakes because of the horses that had won it, because it was a grade II stakes race, and because it carried a $300,000 purse, but it carried a greater significance to me because it was part of the festival of races. It was a big stakes race in our backyard, and I wanted to win it badly.

With Miss Josh's victory in the Violet Handicap, Highland Mills moved into exclusive company. She was one of only some fourteen mares in the world to have two of her offspring win graded/group stakes in 1990, a tremendous achievement, especially considering the obscure stallions she had been bred to. Major farms might have upward of a hundred mares and spend millions on stud fees in a year, yet here we were, with our one mare and chump change. It was very satisfying.

When one is managing a nice horse — not a champion, but a nice stakes winner — discretion is truly the better part of valor. Frankly, there were many stakes races that Joshie could run in, and for people like us who needed to earn money at the races to pay the bills, it was best to run her where she could win. If we were in a situation in which the horse had to run the race of its life just to have a chance to win, we were in the wrong race. Barclay had said we should keep her running in minor stakes in the mid-Atlantic area. Not being asked for 100 percent every time she ran meant she likely would stay sounder and win more often. But the All Along was a special situation, and Barc and I both wanted to run.

Watching the tape of the Violet Handicap over and over, I felt certain I had seen something unexpected and good. Miss Josh had every reason not to win. She just as easily could have been second. After all, Summer Secretary was a seasoned pro and had won three times the money that Joshie had. Miss Josh had won her stakes races on talent.

"My mare ran her race," Jacinto Vasquez had said about Summer Secretary. "She never quits. The other mare had to come and get her."

Horses, as they advance in class in their racing careers, initially win on talent and training. Quite simply, they win because they're better — or better prepared — than the other horses in a race, but at some point a horse will meet another horse in the lane that is equally talented and just as well prepared, and that's when you find out what each is really made of.

Now, watching the race, I could see that somewhere around the sixteenth pole Miss Josh had gone and gotten Summer Secretary. The race had been up for grabs, and Joshie had grabbed it. To me, she became a professional racehorse right there, at the sixteenth pole at The Meadowlands. Now we would see if she could step up her game another notch and take on the toughest field she had ever faced.

Chapter 21

A couple of weeks before the All Along, Barclay called me. "How would you like Laffit Pincay to ride Miss Josh?" he asked. "He's going to be here to ride a horse in the International, and he's looking for rides in the other races."

Barclay didn't have to ask me twice.

"Get him!" I said. And he did. I was ecstatic.

Laffit Pincay had come to the United States from Panama, after signing a jockey contract with owner-breeder Fred Hooper. Hooper had won the Kentucky Derby with the first horse he had ever owned, Hoop, Jr., and remained in racing past the age of one hundred. Early on Pincay earned the reputation for being a strong finisher. It was said — figuratively — that he could pick up a horse and carry it across the finish line. He had won the Kentucky Derby for Claiborne Farm on Swale in 1984 and three Belmont Stakes in a row in the early 1980s. Laffit initially rode in New York, and while there he gave some advice to a young steeplechase rider named Barclay Tagg.

"I would spend a lot of time in the sweat box, trying to lose weight, and he'd come over to me afterward and give me a potassium pill. 'You look terrible,' he'd say. 'Take this. It will make you feel better,'" Barclay remembered.

With his dark hair, his Latin good looks, and his terrific desire to win, Laffit became an immediate fan favorite. He was well liked in the racing community, and respected for his integrity, his discipline, and his immense talent. I was thrilled just thinking that Laffit Pincay was going to ride Miss Josh, who was progressing better than ever.

"Miss Josh is coming into the All Along perfect," Barclay told Tom

Atwell of the *Daily Racing Form*. "She is every bit as good coming into this race as she was when she went into the Violet. In fact, she might be the best she has ever been."

We went to the International party held the night before the race at the Corcoran Gallery in Washington, D.C., and it was a blow-out affair, probably the nicest party I had ever attended. The food was great, the music was wonderful, and all the owners there thought that they could win the next day, including us.

Barclay attended, and he talked to our group.

"If you had to win one race to save your life, and you could choose any jockey, I'd choose Laffit," he said.

I could hardly sleep that night. I was always keyed up the night before a big race, but this seemed to be a race of a different kind, not a different degree. I could barely wait until it was time to get up, get the paper and see what the racing experts thought of our chances, have breakfast, get dressed, and get on the road. I would always rather leave way early and get to the track and have to wait there than to wait at home and then drive like a maniac to the track. I was going to be nervous no matter where I was, and in that situation, I preferred to be at the track.

We had about thirty-five people coming to the race, and we arrived a couple of hours before post time, with Michael on my back in a baby carrier. We were there early enough to see Pincay rate the 17-1 shot Fly Till Dawn just off the early pace in the Budweiser International before sweeping past for an easy victory. I thought that was a good omen.

Five races later we went to the paddock, where I confronted a different atmosphere. Race-day nerves clearly had gotten the better of Barclay and assistant trainer Ronan Cunningham.

"I told you we should keep her in small stakes races," Barclay told me when I got to the stall. I was surprised he would say something like that when it was way too late to do anything.

Looking at the other horses in the race, Cunningham expressed a similar opinion.

"She's in with the gorillas today," he said.

That made me mad.

"Yeah? Well, she's no chimpanzee," I retorted and turned away.

The favorite was Houseproud, a French filly owned by Juddmonte Farms of Prince Khalid Abdullah of Saudi Arabia. She didn't frighten me. She seemed to be a nice filly but not the typical monster that the Europeans usually send over. I thought the trip alone would mean she wouldn't run her usual race, and in that case she wouldn't win. A couple of other European fillies were in the field, but they didn't seem to represent the first team. And, after all, we had the home-field advantage, a considerable asset.

Fieldy — the mare we happily avoided in the Penn National Budweiser Breeders' Cup — was in the race, but I didn't think she could beat us at that point. Again, she was a very nice mare who had made a lot of money because she was so well managed but not a grade I, grade II kind of a mare. The horse that did give me some pause was Foresta, owned by Loblolly Farm and ridden by the ever-cagey Angel Cordero Jr. She had been second in the grade I Flower Bowl at Belmont Park six weeks earlier, and I thought the mile and one-eighth distance would suit her better than the longer Flower Bowl.

Dusk was settling on the late October afternoon as Laffit Pincay walked into the paddock wearing our silks. We shook hands, and I instantly thought, "He has the softest hands I've ever shaken." I don't mean his handshake was weak. It wasn't, but it seemed every section of every finger had extra padding. It was a brief exchange that made a lasting impression.

Miss Josh was doing her "paddock thing" by then, wiggling in the saddling stall, pushing against the groom, eager to get it on. She was on edge but not over the edge. Barclay and Ronan struggled to get her saddled properly, and I smiled as she curled one front leg, a habit of hers. She wasn't trying to paw at the ground, just psyching herself up, I thought. I could see she was ready.

Barclay huddled with Laffit to give him some instructions.

"She's got speed, but don't go to the lead," Barc advised. "Try to get her to settle behind the early pace, and then ask her in the lane. She'll give you everything she's got."

We scurried back to the boxes, and I looked around at the crowd of supporters we had brought to the race with us. On a fall Sunday afternoon, they had each given up what they could have been doing to come see our horse run. That was gratifying. Gus and Sandra Forbush were there. I reflected, "Could it really be four years since this filly was leading the pack of weanlings in the field at Foxhall Farm?"

The horses approached the gate, and one by one they went in. Miss Josh was in the seventh post position in the ten-horse field. The crowd went quiet, as it usually does right before the gates open, and then the horses were off.

Edgar Prado on Iceycindy gunned his filly to the lead, and Laffit followed on Miss Josh. Coming by the stands the first time, she was running second, two lengths behind the leader. Tracking her two lengths farther back was Foresta. Fieldy was well back, and the European horses were trailing.

Iceycindy was in first, a couple of lengths ahead of us around the first turn, but I wasn't worried. We had beaten her easily in the Sensational Handicap in August, and I didn't expect her to put up a fight when the real running started. I turned my binoculars to the toteboard and saw the first half-mile had been run in forty-nine seconds flat on the firm turf course. Right then I knew Miss Josh was going to be tough in the lane.

Prado was trying to ration Iceycindy's speed, but after six furlongs in 1:13 1/5, Laffit had seen enough. He asked Miss Josh, and she responded, cutting into the lead and getting to the flank of Iceycindy in a couple of strides. Miss Josh left Foresta almost four lengths behind as the horses turned for home.

All at once Iceycindy ran out of gas, leaving Miss Josh alone on the lead. Everyone in our group was up and cheering for our girl as she passed the eighth pole with a two-length lead. Foresta had moved into second but was two lengths back and didn't seem to be making up any ground. Then, all at once, she changed leads and began to close. It was one hundred yards to the finish line, and the lead was shrinking fast. Foresta got to the hip, the flank, the neck of Miss Josh, and as the wire flashed by, she put her head down. Photo finish.

The head usher at Laurel came to take us to the winner's circle before the race became official. Around me people were crying and laughing and hugging and kissing. Sandra Forbush came to me weeping for our success and hugged me as I put on the baby carrier with Michael in it and started down the stairs. At that point the track started to show the stretch run on the TV monitors, and I stopped to watch. I saw that one stride before the wire we were ahead, and one stride after the wire we were ahead, but that at the wire, Foresta was fully extended, and Miss Josh was gathering herself for the next stride. We were beaten.

It's hard to feel sorry for oneself after running second in a big race and winning $60,000, and I didn't. It had been a great day, but that fraction of an inch cost us $120,000. When I analyzed the race later, I was really happy. By my calculations, Miss Josh had run two and a half lengths better than she ever had, a considerable improvement. Going into the race, Miss Josh was a nice grade III kind of turf filly. Exiting it, I reckoned that — if she could duplicate the All Along effort — she was capable of running with the best turf mares in the land. Yet, there really was only one way to find out. I decided we would go to California to run in the grade I Matriarch Stakes at Hollywood Park in December.

In between the two races we confronted Michael's pulmonary stenosis. In November the doctors decided that one side of his heart was working harder than normal to push the blood through the smaller opening. They tried to open the valve — a relatively easy procedure — and when the doctor was finished, he came in to see my wife and me.

"I don't think we helped him at all," he said, slumping as he sat down. Rita reached for my hand as the doctor told us, "We're going to have to do open-heart surgery on him."

I wanted the operation done as soon as possible, but the doctors thought we should wait until after Christmas and set the operation for the first week in January.

Preparing for the Matriarch, we confronted another situation. We wanted Laffit to ride Miss Josh, but he had broken his collarbone — for the thirteenth time in his career, I think — and we needed someone else. Barclay and I decided to pick up a rider in California, and we chose Jorge Velasquez, who had ridden Alydar and Pleasant Colony, among a long list of good horses.

We flew Miss Josh to California a couple of days before the race, the first time one of our horses ever had been flown anywhere. She was coming into the race well, and while I respected the field, I wasn't intimidated. Sheikh Mohammed al Maktoum from Dubai had the favored entry in Taffeta and Tulle and Royal Touch, who had been third against Highland Springs in the Breeders' Cup Mile a year earlier. Composer Burt Bacharach had Sweet Roberta. Darby Dan Farm, whose horses I always admired, had Plenty of Grace. The Wildenstein Stable, owner of Steinlen, had Peinture Bleue. And Howard B. Keck, one of Claiborne Farm's clients and the breeder of Le Moulin, the dam of Highland Mills, had Petulia. It was, in other words, a grade I race with grade I owners.

The paddock at Hollywood Park was in front of the grandstand in those days, and as Rita, Michael, and I went down the stairs to go in, a guard stopped us.

"Children can't come into the paddock," he said.

Rita and Michael sat down in an empty box on the first row of the grandstand as I went down the steps. Turning around and looking back up when I reached the paddock, I was entranced by what I saw. Legendary rider Bill Shoemaker, who had won more races than any other jockey in history and who now was a trainer, was standing on the stairs of the grandstand, waving at Michael. Michael smiled at Shoe and waved right back. I would have given anything to have a photograph that captured that moment.

The paddock was a blur to me, though I do remember seeing Burt Bacharach, dressed in jeans and a T-shirt and wearing tennis shoes. Barclay spoke to Velasquez and told him what Miss Josh liked to do. The California bettors didn't think Miss Josh's record amounted to much, sending her off at a healthy 22-1. When they opened the gate, Miss Josh zipped away from the field and took the lead. After an eighth of a mile, I put down my binoculars.

"We'd better enjoy this while we can," I said to Barclay and my sister. I knew she was beaten after she had run a quarter-mile in :23 2/5, and especially when she hit the half-mile in :45 4/5. I had seen the Matchmaker Stakes five months earlier, when she had led from the start, and this one was worse already.

Velasquez said later he couldn't get her to relax. It didn't surprise me. The family tended to be a bit "hot," and all the new surroundings may have worked her up even more.

Out on the course Miss Josh was steaming along with a two-length lead through six furlongs in a zippy 1:09 2/5, sprinting time, and she still had three-eighths of a mile to go. The field caught her on the turn for home, and five horses passed her in the lane. Still, she didn't disgrace herself. She ran a mile in 1:34 flat and finished up the last eighth in less than thirteen seconds. She was beaten about three lengths for everything.

Looking at the race later, I could see a lot to like about her effort. She had traveled three thousand miles and run really well in a grade I event at a different track. She didn't earn any money, but we came away from the race thinking that if we could find a way to get her to settle a bit, she might become a grade I winner in 1991. I had bigger ambitions, however. The past two races had shown me enough to make me believe Miss Josh might be good enough to be the champion turf mare in America, and after we got home I did some research. A couple of weeks later my sister and I went to see Barclay.

I had a list of all the grade I stakes races, their distances, and their locations. We sat down to show them to him and to map out a campaign.

Barc had an objection from the start.

"Where are the mile and a sixteenth races?" he asked.

"There are none," I said. "The shortest grade I is a mile and an eighth, just like the Matriarch."

Barclay expressed an opinion that I shared.

"I think this mare is a miler," he said. "I really don't think that she wants to go any farther than that. Now we may be able to get her to win at a longer distance, but the conditions will have to be right."

We looked at the list of nine races and saw that seven of the grade I races were in California, clearly unfair to horses in the East and clearly out of whack. There was one grade I in Chicago, the Beverly D., and one in New York, the Flower Bowl. Both of those races posed problems for us. The Beverly D. was at a mile and three-sixteenths and the Flower Bowl was at a mile and a quarter. Miss Josh wasn't suited to either. That meant that if she were going to win a grade I stakes race, it was going to have to be in California.

We eliminated a couple of grade I races in California as being too early in the year. Barclay was taking Miss Josh to Florida for the winter, and we weren't going to fly her from there to California to race. I pointed to a race on the list.

"If she's only going to win one grade I, it's going to be this one, the Gamely Handicap the first weekend in June," I said.

Chapter 22

Right after the New Year in 1991, we checked into Georgetown University Hospital for Michael's open-heart surgery. The morning of the operation we three went into the pre-operation room, and Rita and I held Michael while the staff gave him a sedative shot in his thigh. Then he went to sleep and the staff wheeled him into the operating room, with his faithful teddy bear, Ellis, on the gurney with him. Rita and I dissolved into tears. The operation took about four and a half hours, and periodically a nurse would come into the waiting area and tell us that things were going fine. A group of friends, members of the clergy, and family members stayed with us. Some of them had given blood for Michael's operation.

While it may have been routine for the cardiologist, it was the most traumatic event I've ever been through, and Rita felt the same way. I feel for any parent that has to go through that. When I saw Michael strapped to a board, with tubes and wires running from various holes in his body, my first thought was, "He looks like a dissected frog from biology class." He spent the next week in the hospital before returning home to recover.

At the end of the month, we took Michael back for a checkup, and the doctors discovered fluid around his lungs, a fairly normal occurrence. They chose to keep him in the hospital overnight, which meant I had to drive home, pick up clothes for him and us, and drive back to the hospital. When I returned to his floor, Michael was screaming. Every parent knows his or her child's distinctive cry, and Michael's indicated obvious distress. When I got into his room, I could see nurses trying to take blood. They had tried both of his small arms, and having failed they were going to his feet. They tried one, and by the time I arrived, they were on his other foot, poking the needle in and moving it around, searching for his vein. He looked at me with a look that said, "Make them stop!" I held him and the only thing I could think of saying to distract him was, "Michael, next week we're going to Florida, and we're going to see Miss Josh run in the Joe Namath Handicap at Gulfstream Park, and it's going to be so nice and warm and pretty, and we're going to have a wonderful time!"

The distraction worked to some extent. The blood was drawn, and Michael took Lasix for a few days, which removed the fluid from around his lungs. My promise wasn't fulfilled, however. While we did go to Florida, Miss Josh didn't run in the Joe Namath Handicap. It rained, the race was taken off the grass, and we scratched her. We ran her in an allowance race in February, and she was second on yielding turf, a confirmation of the fact that she didn't perform well on turf that wasn't firm. In addition, the saddle slipped under jockey Craig Perret, so her second-place finish was probably better than it looked on paper. A couple of weeks later we were ready to run in the Suwanee River Handicap, and it rained; track officials took it off the grass, and we scratched her again.

On the afternoon of the Suwanee River, however, something happened that changed the way I viewed our girl. I was at the barn, and Barclay and Ronan Cunningham had taken Miss Josh out of the stall to graze her on a patch of grass growing between her barn and the next one. Sitting in a lawn chair, I watched her tear at the grass, keeping her head low to the ground while eating contentedly. In those days the barns at Gulfstream were separated from the racetrack by a tall, thick hedge. One couldn't see through the bushes, but the sounds of the races could be heard clearly.

I was just sitting there, lazing in the afternoon sun, when the horses came out for the next race on the card. When they galloped past, warming up, Miss Josh heard them. She picked her head up and uttered a sound I had never heard from a horse before. She didn't whinny at them, and she didn't nicker. She growled at them, a low, guttural sound, something like what a cougar might make, and that brought me out of my chair. Then she began to get all revved up, rearing and lunging against the shank, showing her eagerness to get at those horses. Barclay yelled, "Get her back into the barn! You won't be able to control her if you don't!"

I was stunned as they led her back into the quiet of the late afternoon shed row and then into her stall. She calmed down quickly, but that moment taught me everything I ever would need to know about that mare.

Miss Josh didn't simply want to defeat other horses. She wanted to dominate them, to destroy them. She had become a warrior. That's when I decided to try her against colts in the mile and a sixteenth, grade II Canadian Club Turf Handicap at Gulfstream. To win that, all she would have to do would be to defeat Izvestia, the 1990 Canadian Horse of the Year and winner of Canada's Triple Crown, and another dozen stakes colts. That's all.

I approached Barclay with the idea, and while he initially opposed it, he gradually came around. Or maybe he agreed just to get me to stop bugging him. In any case, we aimed for the Canadian Club Turf Handicap on March 9. Given the money and the weight allowance she would receive from the boys, the venture seemed worth the risk, particularly since Gulfstream had scheduled no other filly and mare stakes races on the turf other than one at a mile and a half, too far for her.

Miss Josh looked great in the paddock that day, but my heart was pounding. I had never run a female against males before, especially in a grade II stakes race. I thought she could beat Izvestia on grass, yet he wasn't the only one she had to beat. She also was in against colts like Noble Savage, owned by Sheikh Mohammed al Maktoum of Dubai; Yonder, owned by Canadian industrialist Frank Stronach; Ole Atocha, owned by Allaire du Pont; and others. Even if Izvestia weren't in the field, it wasn't going to be a cakewalk.

Dave Penna, who had never ridden Miss Josh before, was our jockey, and when Barclay threw him on, I said the same thing I said to all jockeys that rode our horses: "Good luck, and have a good, safe trip."

It was a crapshoot coming out of the gate. Penna steered Miss Josh toward the rail well before the first turn, and she was sixth, six lengths behind the leader, when they straightened out for the run down the backstretch. Penna saw a small opening along the rail and tried to squeeze through it, but another horse came over, and he had to take hold of Miss Josh. With a half-mile to run, Miss Josh was fifth and moving up again.

On the final turn Penna had her on the rail, the shortest way to the finish line. He asked her again, and again a horse came over and closed her off. So far, there was no good luck, and the trip she was getting seemed decidedly unsafe. With a quarter-mile to go, and with her on the rail, a horse cut to the inside so quickly that Penna had to snatch the reins. Miss Josh's mouth flew open, her head came straight up, and I lost sight of her. She was a brown face in amongst a mass of other brown faces, and when I couldn't pick out her — or our chocolate and pink silks — I thought that she had gone over the rail. I looked into the infield to see if she were thrashing around there, saw nothing, and turned to Barclay.

"Barc, did she fall?" I asked. He said nothing. He was focusing his binoculars on the stretch. I turned back to the race to discover that instead of falling, she had righted herself, accelerated instantly, and had the lead with an eighth of a mile to go.

Izvestia was a length and a half behind and closing furiously. Miss Josh was along the rail, fighting on. Finally, in the last fifty yards, Izvestia caught up and went past her to win by a neck. We were second.

I had an odd feeling after the race. I was incredibly proud of her effort. Yet, at the same time, I felt the race could have been ours, should have been ours. It was the roughest-run race that one of our horses ever was in, and I think if she had not been stopped at the top of the lane, we would have won.

I had a call waiting for me when I got home from Florida. It was Duncan Taylor. He had sold us Highland Mills, and he always had been quick with some help or advice whenever we asked. Now he was interested in the daughter of the filly he had sold us eleven years earlier.

"Would you be interested in selling Miss Josh?" he asked.

"How much do you have in mind?" I replied.

"Five-hundred-thousand dollars," he said.

I was flattered. We had paid $6,500 for her stud fee, and with the second-place money in the Canadian Club Turf Handicap, she had just topped $300,000 in earnings. Now a professional horseman whose advice I trusted was trying to buy our girl for a half-million dollars. It was a heady invitation, but one I quickly turned down. She was a special mare to me, and I thought she was on the verge of having a great year.

Duncan understood.

"Now don't come to me telling me you're out of money in six months," he closed with a laugh.

Money was a constant concern with us. Even though we had won more than $300,000 in 1990, we were supporting a number of horses. We had Highland Mills, her babies, and her stud fees, and a three-year-old filly, Highland Crystal, who hadn't earned a dollar. We also had a two-year-old colt named Royal Mountain Inn who wouldn't get to the races for another year. And at the stakes level, we were in against people with nearly unlimited cash to fulfill their equine ambitions.

That fact became clear to me one afternoon in Kentucky, as we looked at stallions. We were on a farm owned by one of the sheikhs from Dubai, and the place was immaculate. Every blade of grass was manicured, every piece of brass was polished, and swans swam in the manmade ponds.

Riding in a golf cart with the farm manager, I came up with a question. Because the stable did most of its racing in Europe, I wondered what they did with the young horses they bred in Kentucky.

"Do you break your yearlings here and then ship them to Europe, or do you send them all over there to be broken?" I asked.

"We fly them all over there to be broken," the farm manager replied. Then he added casually, "Last year we had 279 yearlings."

That comment hung in the air. I thought, "Last year we had one yearling, and if our one is any good, he'll have to go against the best of your 279."

It hardly seems a fair contest, but that's the way it is in the horse business. The game cuts you no slack. There isn't a "Kentucky Derby for owners with three or fewer horses." There is the Kentucky Derby. Come and get it, if you can.

The slogan I had used for the first decade in the business had said it all: "Dedicated to breeding and racing the Champion." I had found Lucy's Axe and had come up with Highland Springs, the best runner that stallion ever sired. Then we had bred Millsie to Nasty and Bold, a stallion whom I admired and respected, and had come up with Miss Josh. I went to Raise a Man, thinking I would inject some speed into the pedigree, and then I went to Vigors, a big, robust stallion who had been the best runner of the group. That mating had given us Royal Mountain Inn.

The reports about Highland Crystal and Royal Mountain Inn were uniformly good, though we did have a scare.

When Royal Mountain Inn was being broken, he stumbled a time or two when coming in from the track. They brought in a veterinarian, and he had a quick diagnosis: wobbles.

Hearing your horse has wobbles is about the worst news an owner can receive. This disease of the spinal column interferes with the signals from the brain to the hind end. A horse with wobbles will not be coordinated enough to walk, let alone run. A racehorse with wobbles has a death sentence.

We all went to see the horse and speak with the vet. Barclay went with us. While my sister and I stood and talked to the vet, Barclay took Royal Mountain Inn by the shank and backed him up the length of the shed row. Then he turned him in a tight circle over and over again. After a couple of minutes of this, he came over to us.

"I don't know what this horse has, but he doesn't have wobbles. Of that I'm certain," Barclay said.

The vet asked him how he could be so positive.

"I just turned him around and backed him up, and he couldn't do that if he had wobbles."

Royal Mountain Inn never stumbled like that again, but it's a good example of the kinds of situations horse owners face every day. Even if you've bred a great horse, there is no guarantee it won't get the wobbles or develop breathing problems or chip a knee or ankle or fall prey to a hundred other maladies and conditions that competitive horses are prone to. Royal Mountain Inn looked like he had talent, but that didn't mean he couldn't be injured. He might never run, just like any other racehorse. Overcoming those odds was part of what made having a good horse so rewarding.

Meanwhile, after the debacle of the Canadian Club Turf Handicap, we gave Miss Josh almost a month to recover before asking her to run against colts again, this time in the mile and a sixteenth Fort Lauderdale Handicap. The field didn't have Izvestia, but it still carried a purse of $100,000, and it still was against the colts. That made it tough enough.

Dave Penna was back in the irons when they sprung the gate, and Miss Josh broke badly. She threw her head in the air and was dead last out of the gate. She was rank along the rail, and Penna had to steady her on the second turn. By the time they hit the head of the stretch, she had been left with too much to do. She had to find three lengths in the lane, and she did just that, getting up to win in the absolute last stride. Looking at the photo of the race, it seems to me that she's gritting her teeth in the final strides.

According to the timer, the last sixteenth of a mile was run in six seconds, which meant that Miss Josh ran it in five seconds and change. I hand-timed the last eighth of a mile as best I could by using the video of the race, and it kept pointing to one thing: Miss Josh had run the last eighth of a mile in less than eleven seconds, which is simply incredible.

Chapter **23**

*M*iss Josh returned to Maryland in the middle of April 1991 as the most accomplished turf mare in the East, at that point. After beating colts in the Fort Lauderdale, we entered her in the grade III Gallorette Handicap at Pimlico. Coming up to the race, she worked a half-mile in a reported fifty-four seconds, which is very slow, especially for stakes horses. There was nothing wrong with her, however. It's just that she simply found some training boring. She had developed a thirst for competition, and when it wasn't there — Barclay always worked her by herself — she just didn't seem to care one way or the other how she worked.

I caught the workout as it was listed in the *Racing Form*, and when I asked Barclay about it, he said they had it all wrong.

"She didn't work a half-mile in fifty-four seconds," he said. "She worked it in about a minute."

It didn't bother me at all. I never was one who put a lot of stock into how fast a horse worked in the morning. Of course, if she or any other horse we owned worked a half-mile in forty-five seconds or so consistently, I certainly wouldn't have been disappointed. Owners thrive on good news about their horses, but Miss Josh usually didn't work fast, so with her, I had to get my kicks when she ran.

The Gallorette was the first stakes race on the grass for fillies and mares north of Florida, and with two tough stakes races against colts under her belt already, I wanted to give her an easy race. When we got to the paddock, I pointed out to my sister that Miss Josh was favored at 1-5.

"It's been a long time since we've had a horse at 1-5 in a graded stakes race," I said. "In fact, we've never had a horse at 1-5 in a graded stakes race."

The Gallorette featured mostly turf mares making their first starts of the year, while Miss Josh already had been battle-tested. She would have to throw in a clunker to give the others a chance. Jockey Edgar Prado had her sitting just off a soft early pace, and when he asked her to run, she easily motored past the leader. In the stretch Barc's other horse, Splendid Try, put in a run and got within a couple of lengths of Miss Josh — which gave me momentary pause, but Miss Josh held her stablemate safe by a length and three-quarters.

After the race Prado expressed little concern, when asked about Splendid Try's rally.

"Were you worried when she got so close?" Pimlico's handicapper asked the jockey in an interview for the track's telecast.

"Not really," Prado answered nonchalantly. "I had plenty of horse."

The victory in the Gallorette set matters on course for the grade I Gamely Handicap at Hollywood Park the first Sunday in June. Win that, and we could start talking about the Eclipse Award as the best turf mare in America.

What most people don't realize is that at some point horses hit a level beyond which they never go. There are horses that finish second and third in several stakes races without winning even one. There are stakes winners that cannot become graded stakes winners, grade III winners that cannot win grade II races, and so on. At the peak are the grade I winners. There's an old saying in racing that grade I races are won by grade I horses. Miss Josh had won two grade III stakes races, but in her three attempts at grade II races, she had two seconds and a sixth to show for her efforts. In her only attempt at a grade I stakes race — the Matriarch Handicap, over the same turf course as the Gamely — she had been sixth. In spite of her recent record against colts, in spite of my opinion that she seemed a better horse than she had been in her first grade I race, the fact remained that she still had to go out there and do it.

Then there were the famous Beyer speed figures — originated by Andy Beyer, a Harvard English major who developed a way to figure out how fast a horse actually had run in a race by taking into account how slow or fast a track might have been. According to his figures, Miss Josh was about two lengths slower than Fire the Groom and a couple of other California mares. I had watched those turf mares all winter and spring, and I concluded that the figures leading to that considerable deficit had to be wrong. I had reviewed every race that every one of the important contenders had run, studied the charts, dissected the results, and come to the conclusion their Beyer figures were too high, and I was willing to stake Miss Josh's reputation on that.

Barclay Tagg is conservative by nature, even pessimistic, but he was committed early on to going to the Gamely. What I couldn't get him to commit to was staying out there an additional three weeks to run in the Beverly Hills Handicap, another grade I turf stakes race, if she lost the Gamely. It seemed quite clear to me that the Gamely was her shot. If she couldn't handle the opposition in that race, it wasn't likely she would ever run in another grade I stakes. The pressure was on.

We got a flight for Joshie to California on the Thursday evening before the race on Sunday. It left from Newark, and, to our surprise and chagrin, included a change of planes in Detroit in the middle of the night. As it turned out, she settled down when they put her on the second plane and slept the rest of the way.

That night a strange thing happened. For no apparent reason I awoke out of a deep sleep at about 2 a.m. I had heard no sound, seen no lights. I checked the clock, and then I remembered Miss Josh was on the plane right then. My subconscious knew that, and lying awake in the dark, my brain produced the running of the race, an occurrence I would experience before every remaining race in her career. I could "see" the race, see Miss Josh lying off the early pace and then powering to victory in the stretch. I came to enjoy those pre-dawn visions. It made me feel very close to the horses.

When the van arrived at the airport to take Miss Josh to Hollywood Park, assistant trainer Ronan Cunningham noticed her Jockey Club papers — the official papers that identify a Thoroughbred — were missing. Without those, she could not run in the Gamely, nor in any other race for that matter. A trainer-friend in California said when he saw Ronan, the assistant trainer was absolutely white with fear. "It's only a horse race," the friend advised. Not long after, the phone rang. Cleaning up the plane after the flight, the crew had found the papers. No harm was done. Still, when you're trying to do something you haven't done before, you want everything to be perfect, and the flight and the missing papers put us all on edge.

Because of Miss Josh's presence, the Los Angeles papers seemed to be paying more attention to the Gamely than they otherwise might have. The reporters were playing up the East versus West dynamic. One reporter — after saying that Fire the Groom had won five stakes races in a row, while Little Brianne had posted "overpowering" upsets over champion Bayakoa at Santa Anita — wrote that, "The new face in the cast belongs to Miss Josh, who is traveling 3,000 miles for the privilege of running against this pair."

One thing in our favor, however, was having Laffit Pincay back in the saddle; I felt sure that he would give her a good ride.

I arrived at Hollywood Park on Saturday afternoon, and Barclay already was there. He had seen the advance editions of the *Racing Form* and the *Racing Times*, and his nerves were getting the better of him. He had seen the Beyer speed figures by then, and he could see that — at least according to them — Miss Josh didn't quite match up. He was grousing about going so far just to be beaten, but I let it pass. When he told me she had settled into her stall well and was eating well, it was all I needed to hear. At that point I was willing to take a stand with our girl. Andy Beyer's figures were wrong, I said. "And you'll all see that tomorrow afternoon."

Chapter 24

Sunday dawned bright and cool, a terrific June day in California. Barclay and I went to the track early to see Miss Josh and to do a couple of little things.

Miss Josh looked great. She had eaten her breakfast first thing in the morning and had taken a jog on the track. Now she was preparing for a nap.

Although Bonner and Tom, as well as some other partners, were with me, my wife and son hadn't made the trip, and my mother was in Georgia at a family reunion. I knew my mother would go to a small, old church that she attended in her youth. She said later she had added Miss Josh to her prayer list that morning. I went back to the hotel, had a little break-fast, read the local papers, and talked with the fifteen other people who had come from the East Coast to see our horse run. Finally it was time to get dressed and go to the track.

When we arrived at Hollywood Park, we were escorted to the director's room on an upper floor of the grandstand. The staff had laid out two tables for us, with ribbons in our racing colors running the length of both tables. There was a complete buffet, with a wide variety of foods, down to a make-your-own-sundae bar. With my system still on Eastern time, for once I was able to eat something before a big race. In fact, I had quite a meal, which was very unusual for me.

I looked around the room and it dawned on me the people at the other tables — which also had colored ribbons on them — were owners of the other horses in the Gamely Handicap.

Sitting one table away from us was Clarence Scharbauer, a Texan who had bought Alysheba as a yearling colt for $500,000 in 1985 and won the

Kentucky Derby and Preakness Stakes with him in 1987 and the Breeders' Cup Classic in 1988. I'm not certain why Scharbauer was there — maybe he was lending moral support to his trainer, Jack Van Berg, who had Little Brianne in the race — but we struck up a conversation. I had enjoyed Scharbauer's comments and style from afar when his wife and daughter were racing Alysheba, and he was just as warm in person. He had claimed to be "just a chore boy" when Alysheba was winning all his races and all his money.

When Alysheba retired from racing, Scharbauer sent him to Lane's End Farm, owned by his friend Will Farish, who would become America's ambassador to Great Britain under President George W. Bush. Farish was a personal friend of Queen Elizabeth II and kept some of her mares at his place. Approximately once a year the queen would visit Kentucky to see her mares and inspect some stallions. On her latest trip, she had seen Alysheba, and Scharbauer shared the story with us.

"Yeah, I got a call from Will (Farish) the other day," Scharbauer drawled, "and he said that she had seen my horse and liked him, and could she breed a mare to him for free? I said, 'Hell, no! She's got more money than I do, let her pay like everybody else!'"

The afternoon dragged until it finally was time for us to go to the paddock and see Miss Josh get saddled. We met Barclay there, and Ronan Cunningham brought in our girl. Her coat gleamed in the bright sunshine, and as they saddled her, she began her little dance, wiggling this way and that, making life hard for Barclay as he struggled to get her to stand still long enough to saddle her properly.

While watching Joshie take a few turns in the walking ring, I mentioned to my sister a realization I'd had.

"Did you know that we've won a race on this day for two years running?" I pronounced. "Not the date, but the first Sunday in June. Highland Springs won that claiming race two years ago, and Miss Josh won her first race on the grass last year on this day."

I was saving another realization until after we won, if we won. It was two years to the day since Miss Josh had won her first race, a $12,000 maiden claimer. Her journey from $12,000 maiden claimer to graded stakes winner, while not unprecedented, still was a phenomenal achievement. Maiden claimers that do that generally can be counted on the fingers of one hand, and we already had campaigned two. Most of the time a good horse is good from the very beginning of its racing career, but Highland Springs and Miss Josh had shown that good horses could make a long, long climb from obscurity to the upper echelons of the game.

Standing in the Hollywood Park paddock, I thought of my friend Cot Campbell of Dogwood Stable. His Summer Squall had won the 1990 Preakness, and less than a month earlier he had been the featured speaker at the Virginia Thoroughbred Association's annual awards dinner. Cot and I had chatted before the speech.

"How's your big horse, the one that won at Saratoga?" Cot asked me.

"Well, he's retired," I answered.

"Oh, that's a shame," he said, and we chatted some more. "Do you have any other good horses coming along?"

"We have Miss Josh," I said, "his half sister."

"You own Miss Josh?" he asked, tilting his head as if he were surprised. "It looks like she's a very nice mare."

It's an interesting thing, the friendships that develop among owners. Horse racing is a cutthroat business; when one owner wins, several others lose and leave the race with no money in their pockets. Still, I always found other owners very supportive. When we won, I almost always got congratulatory messages and calls from people in the business, which made the victories that much sweeter. The respect of one's peers, after all, is a very special commodity.

With fourteen minutes to the post, Laffit Pincay came into the paddock and walked over to greet us. It was great to see him in our silks again. Then he went and conferred with Barclay, while my sister and I checked out the competition, especially Fire the Groom, the one on a winning streak that stretched back to her racing days in England. She looked good, we thought, and her pedigree was very attractive. She could run. I knew that, both from her record and from my research.

The paddock judge called, "Riders up," and the jockeys mounted and headed toward the track. Ronan had Miss Josh's shank and walked beside her. Ronan said later that he was on a mission. Miss Josh had been beaten the last time she had showed up at Hollywood Park in a grade I stakes race.

People who work with horses naturally identify with them. The horses become theirs, no matter what The Jockey Club papers say. Grooms and hot walkers and exercise riders and assistant trainers and trainers get great psychological rewards when one of their horses goes out and does something spectacular. Ronan thought "his" horse was ready.

We decided we wouldn't go back into the Director's Room to watch the race. We were afraid we might scream too loudly for those decorous premises, and we especially didn't want to get out of hand in front of the people who owned the other mares in the field. Actually, we did want to get out of hand. That would mean that Miss Josh was running well. We just didn't want to do it in front of the other horse owners, so we went into the grandstand and stood in the aisle, just like ordinary racing fans, except we were all dressed up for the occasion.

Track announcer Trevor Denman had been going through the introductions of the mares while we got situated, and I could see Miss Josh start taking small nips at the mane of her lead pony. The introductions over, she broke off and galloped around the track and onto the backstretch. I had taken my binoculars out of their case and placed the case at my feet, up against the rail post. Barclay and my sister were down the aisle to the left of me. I didn't know where the other people were. I was in a world of my own, totally focused on our girl.

The horses finished their warm-ups and started onto the turf course and into the gate. To speed things up, the gate crew loaded two mares at a time, and Miss Josh, being number six, was the last of the eleven to load. She was eager in the gate and stuck her nose right up into the V-shape that the gates make when the doors are closed.

When the horses broke from the gate, I found myself in a trance. I was supremely aware of what was going on in the race, but I couldn't begin to tell you what was going on around me or anywhere else in the world for that matter. I watched the race in what seemed like slow motion, and I knew everything that was happening around that racecourse. What I didn't know at the time was that I was about to witness the most professional, the most competent, the most outstanding piece of race riding any jockey would ever give a horse of ours.

You see, Miss Josh wanted to be a sprinter. Her idea of a race was to burst out of the gate as quickly as she could and run as hard as she could as far as she could. She was designed to run six- or seven-furlongs on the dirt, but her poor feet prevented that. We were going against her breeding and her body type when we asked her to run a quarter-mile or farther than she wanted to go on the grass. The only way she could possibly win under those conditions was to have a great rider on her back, and in Laffit, she did.

I saw the filly Freya Stark take the early lead and sprint away from the field. I saw the multiple grade I winner Little Brianne and the longshot Dead Heat follow her, and I could see Laffit take hold of Miss Josh and ease her back into fourth as they came out of the chute in the infield and began their run around the first turn. Track announcer Trevor Denman called out, "the pace is just a steady one, not fast, but not that slow," and I took a quick peek at the timer and saw they had gone the first quarter-mile in :23 3/5. Miss Josh was about three lengths back at that point, so she had done her quarter in a bit more than twenty-four seconds. Another quarter-mile with fractions like that one, and she would come up big in the stretch. Of that I was certain.

Laffit had her off the rail in fourth place in the run down the backside. He was sitting coolly in the saddle. He had a hold of her, and she was snug against the bit, and together the two made a threatening presence. Freya Stark had managed to keep the lead while slowing the pace down. When they passed the first half-mile, the timer reported the good news — :48 1/5 — and Miss Josh was still two lengths back. I knew we were alive.

I took a look at the back of the pack and found Fire the Groom running next to last. She appeared to be about six or seven lengths behind us, but a stretch runner by habit, she was where I expected her to be. I wasn't concerned about any other horse, and I swung my binoculars back to the leaders and watched as Laffit gradually eased Miss Josh up toward the front. This would be no breathtaking move, not like the one she had made in the Violet Handicap nine months earlier. Inch by inch, Laffit gently allowed her to advance.

With three-eighths of a mile left to run, he let out a notch, and she moved to the leaders, but she still wasn't full out. Meanwhile, Gary Stevens on Fire the Groom got busy at the back of the pack.

Denman called out, "Fire the Groom has ten lengths to make up!"

Trevor must have been seeing things that day. Fire the Groom was more like three lengths behind the leader, only two behind our girl.

"They are homeward bound … Freya Stark, Dead Heat, Miss Josh … Fire the Groom finding room and flying in the red colors!"

There may have been a hurricane approaching from behind, but Laffit didn't panic. He wasn't going to move to the front too soon. Finally, inside the eighth pole, with 150 yards to run, he decided it was time. He turned his stick up and popped Miss Josh, who immediately stepped up her pace to edge past her competition.

"Fire the Groom coming flying, but Miss Josh has the lead!"

Time was rapidly running out. Trevor saw and called the move that Island Jamboree was making from the back of the pack. At the sixteenth pole Joshie was being sandwiched. Island Jamboree was outside her, and Fire the Groom was coming hard at her from the inside.

"Keep her coming!" I shouted. "All the way home!"

Laffit hit her twice right-handed and switched the stick to his left hand and waved it in front of her left eye. He didn't hit her again. He didn't have to. She was giving him everything she had, everything that had been bred into her, everything that Barclay had trained into her, and Laffit knew it. Just a little farther, maybe about as far as the run from home plate to first base. If she held on just that little bit more, the victory would be ours.

"Miss Josh hanging on …"

Fire the Groom's stretch run was faltering. She and Island Jamboree could get no farther than Laffit's boots. It was over.

"Miss Josh has won it in a driving finish from Island Jamboree and Fire the Groom!"

It's odd, really, the things that happen when something as emotional as Miss Josh's win occurs. Down the aisle my sister was looking for me, sobbing. She couldn't find me. I had other matters to deal with. At some point during the race, I had kicked my binoculars case into the box in front of me, and when I spotted it, I asked the people sitting there to hand it over to me. They had the oddest looks on their faces, and my senses were all messed up. I honestly could not tell if I was whispering or shouting, but they hesitated. They finally handed it to me so gingerly one would have thought they were passing over a beaker of nitroglycerin.

My sister gave up her quest to find me and headed toward the winner's circle, steadying herself on Barclay's arm.

"Your brother was right; he was right," Barclay kept saying to her.

The binoculars case secured, I bounded down the stairs. Suddenly, I had the oddest physical reaction I'd ever had in my life. I felt like a thousand needles were sticking my skin from the inside. It was extremely unpleasant, but it passed quickly. Still, it had to be some incredible combination of chemicals that my brain had dumped into my system at that moment.

There were hugs and tears all around in the winner's circle, and then Laffit brought Miss Josh in, and the first words out of his mouth were, "Don't run her here again. It was too hard on her. The track was stinging her feet all the way around, and she didn't like it at all."

When I heard that, I was stunned.

"You mean to tell me," I thought, "that we shipped her three thousand miles, upset her entire routine, and faced the best turf mares in the West, and she didn't like the turf course, and she still won? Just how tough is this mare?"

We all went back to the Director's Room. R.D. Hubbard came in and opened a bottle of champagne and toasted our win. Then we watched the race a time or two as we celebrated our victory. When we decided to leave, I caught a ride with my sister and brother-in-law. After we got into the car and closed the doors, I couldn't hold in my emotions any longer.

"I knew she could beat those sons-of-bitches!"

Chapter 25

Winning the Gamely Handicap took Miss Josh to a new level, and Barclay, too. It was his first grade I victory, making the victory even more special for us. Barclay had not complained about what life had given him. He wasn't the kind of trainer to get the rich owner with millions of dollars to spend on untested yearlings every year, and he had labored almost unnoticed in racing's vineyards for decades. Now he had a grade I winner, and we had put it in his stable. As much as winning the Gamely, the idea we had helped a good man get some well-deserved recognition was extremely satisfying.

Now racing writers were mentioning Miss Josh and the Eclipse Award in the same sentence. Everything we had done so far that year had led us to that point, but we had more than six months to go. We had to keep moving forward.

Miss Josh was hobbling by the time she got to the test barn after the Gamely. The adrenaline of the race had worn off, and Ronan and Barclay could see the discomfort had surpassed her high threshold for pain. She gradually recovered from her sore feet and shipped home a couple of days later. I was there when she arrived at Barclay's barn, in the middle of a lovely June afternoon. The track was quiet, and many of the horses were asleep in their stalls when the van arrived. The doors opened, and she came out, looking absolutely magnificent. People often ask whether a horse knows when it wins a race. One look at Miss Josh, and you could see she understood what she had done. She arched her neck, put her tail up, and came down the hill, punching the ground like she was driving nails. When she got to the corner of the barn, she let out a loud whinny that brought every head out of every stall. To me it seemed like she was declaring, "I told you I was going out there to win, and I did!"

Laffit's advice about Miss Josh's feet and the Hollywood Park turf course threw a wrench into our plans. We had thought we might return to that track for the grade I Beverly Hills Handicap three weeks later or for the grade I Matriarch Handicap in December, but after seeing her so lame, both races were out. We knew that she wouldn't win the grade I Yellow Ribbon Stakes at Santa Anita or the grade I Flower Bowl at Belmont Park. Both were at a mile and a quarter, way too far for her. We considered the Breeders' Cup Mile, whose distance really suited her, but we had a little problem. Laffit was riding a colt named Tight Spot, the leading turf male in America, and Tight Spot, who was aiming for the Mile. I didn't want to have to get another rider.

That left just two grade I possibilities, the mile and an eighth Ramona Handicap at Del Mar in California and the mile and three-sixteenths Beverly D. Stakes at Arlington Park in Chicago. If we went to Del Mar, we would be in the position of having to fly to California to race against the local mares. I wasn't sure I wanted to give Fire the Groom and others that advantage again. At least, if we ran in Chicago — even though the race seemed a tad too long for her — the California mares would have to ship in just like we did, and so we penciled in that race, scheduled for the end of August. We just needed to get from where we were to there.

When we began the year, I had been certain of one thing: We would not run Miss Josh in the grade II Matchmaker Stakes at Atlantic City. Considering how she had run the year before, I wasn't sure she was suited for the mile and three-sixteenths distance. Yet, I knew that sometimes a horse can win at longer distances if it is the best in the field and if it is properly ridden. After watching Laffit's masterful ride in the Gamely, I felt confident the ride would be fine. We decided to go, with Laffit aboard, the first time in thirteen years he had ridden at

Atlantic City Race Course.

Miss Josh clearly was the most accomplished horse in the field. The turf was firm, the field was small — only six others, and she came into the race well. Unlike her usual antics before a race, Miss Josh was absolutely dead calm when she was being saddled. I wasn't certain that was a good thing. I couldn't tell if she had brought her A game or if our dreams of winning a championship were about to be dashed right there in Atlantic City.

That question was answered quickly as she broke from the gate well and sat outside, just behind the leaders as they went into the first turn. When I saw how eager she was, my worries vanished. For the first time in a long time, I could just sit back and enjoy the race. The track announcer gave a wonderful call, focusing on our girl, calling her the "highweight" and the "public choice," which she decidedly was at 1-2 odds. On the last turn, Christiecat, the leader at that point, was "asked to fend off Miss Josh." When Laffit saw it was time to go, he asked Miss Josh for run, and she accelerated away from the field instantly, opening up four lengths or so before going back to her old habit of thinking the race over and slowing down. Laffit flicked her lightly with the whip, and she easily held off Barclay's other entrant, Whip Cream.

After the race we were whisked off to the press box. I started the interview by telling the reporters about how small an outfit we were, with only one broodmare, and I ended with, "We've been really lucky."

From behind me someone said, "It doesn't sound like luck to me."

It was one of those moments where you feel like you need to respond, and I was struggling with a rejoinder. My brain fumbled for a moment, and then it came to me. All I had to do was to think about what Paul Mellon — who lived in the same county as I did — had done with his horses.

"Well, Mr. Mellon bred the dam and the granddam and owned the great-granddam of the great Mill Reef," I said. "When we've done something like that, then I'll say it wasn't luck."

Steve Haskin, then writing for *Daily Racing Form*, had cornered my mother — the original Miss Josh — and she was regaling him with our roller-coaster ride in the horse business. Then, looking at me being interviewed, she said something priceless.

"You know, I told George that if he had studied law the way he studies bloodlines, he'd be a Supreme Court justice by now," she said.

For his part, Laffit Pincay had some nice words to tell the reporters about Miss Josh.

"She's become very special to me, and I'd go anywhere to ride her," he said.

Miss Josh had won four stakes races in a row so far in 1991, and it was only July 3. Two years earlier on that date we won our first stakes race with Highland Springs. Now, we had just taken our eleventh stakes race. It had been an incredible run, especially when one considers we had done it with two horses, both out of the same mare.

And it didn't seem that the gravy train was about to come to a screeching halt any time soon. Highland Crystal was about to go to the races, and she seemed to have ability. Waiting in the wings was the two-year-old Royal Mountain Inn, a giant gray whose claim to fame at that point was that he shared the same birthday as Miss Josh.

After the Matchmaker we started getting calls from representatives from Ascot Race Course in England. Wanting to encourage international racing, they invited Miss Josh to run in the group I Queen Elizabeth II Stakes in September.

"We'll fly you, your family, the trainer, the jockey, the horse over here and pay all your expenses while you're here," one representative said.

The race was at a mile, and while I was somewhat tempted, it would have been too much to ask her to race on an undulating course and around a right turn after spending her life turning left on a flat course. I also didn't think she would have time to acclimate before the race. Then they added one final sweetener.

"Of course, if you were to win, you understand that the queen would give you the trophy," they told me.

When my mother heard that, she said we ought to go. But I explained how our plan didn't include a trip to England. She accepted the decision.

We were about to enter dangerous waters. I knew that traditionally the people who vote for the Eclipse Award give more weight to races won late in the year than those won in the first half, and while Miss Josh was the pro-tem leader for the Eclipse Award, matters were about to get more serious.

After talking with just about everybody we knew in the sport, we decided to put up the $40,000 supplemental fee to run in the Beverly D. Stakes. We knew it would be asking a lot from Miss Josh to run that far against the kind of horse the race likely would attract, yet she had just won the Matchmaker Stakes at the same distance. Maybe she could do it again.

Bloodstock agent Russell Jones, who owned Joshie's younger half sister, Ferebee, doubted our mare's ability to win. When I said she had just won at the distance, he retorted, "The difference between the horses she just beat and the horses she'll face in Chicago is the difference between chicken poop and chicken salad," though he didn't use the word "poop."

The deciding factor for me, however, was my belief that major races in the fall were not going to go our way. Other horses would be winning the Yellow Ribbon and Matriarch, and they would attract attention from voters right when they would be casting their ballots. I thought what we needed to do was to finish the campaign right there, in Chicago. If she could win her fifth straight stakes race, and, especially, her second grade I stakes, I thought the voters would look at her record at that point and say, "Well, she's the best turf mare in America," no matter who won the later grade I races.

"We're going to Chicago," I told my sister and everybody else. "We're going to win the Beverly D. We're going to wrap up the Eclipse Award before September."

We had one more mountain to climb, and it was at Arlington Park in Chicago.

"The stone that the builders rejected has become the chief cornerstone."
Psalm 118:22

Having a mare like Highland Mills put us in an interesting situation. In the beginning she had been an irritant, a constant nagging reminder of my failures. She had been such an extraordinarily useless racehorse that I was certain I didn't want to be around her. I was determined to sell her, but Tyson Gilpin talked me out of it. I then watched in amazement as she began to produce good horse after good horse. It became evident after her first two foals that she was our best broodmare. And after the first three foals resulted in three stakes horses, breeders began to contact me about buying her. The irony was that in 1985 I would have sold her for almost any price. Now, six years later, I didn't even give the callers the opportunity to say how much they were willing to pay for her.

All the big farms in the business contacted us. When we started hearing from English and Irish bloodstock agents, I started to wonder whom they were representing. Arab sheikhs? British moguls? Irish tax exiles? I really didn't know. All I knew was that to any of them, she would be just another mare in a field populated with maybe one hundred other mares. To us, she was everything, the only reason we were still in the business.

The calls from overseas went like this:

"Mr. Rowand," a person, usually with a British accent, would say, "I'm calling to see if you'd be interested in selling your mare."

"Well, thank you for your interest, but she's not for sale," I'd respond quickly.

"Oh, why don't you put a price on her, and let's see where that goes," a few responded.

"Okay, how about a hundred million dollars? That's a price!" I once thought about saying, but didn't. I'd been brought up better than that, so I would just repeat, "Thank you, but she's just not for sale."

About this same time I noticed that trying to win an Eclipse Award wasn't much fun. We had taken on stiff challenges, shipped coast to coast, run against colts twice, and we weren't finished. The pressure never decreased. In fact, after every win it seemed to increase. We thought we had to win out, that she couldn't afford even one stumble, and in Chicago waited Fire the Groom again, and a new shooter, the European runner Colour Chart, owned by Sheikh Mohammed of Dubai.

Miss Josh received considerable press going into the race. Ray Paulick wrote in the *Racing Times* that after her wins in Florida, Maryland, California, and New Jersey, her "nationwide campaign could be conceived as an orchestration for an Eclipse Award … Miss Josh is the clear leader at present, and a win in the Beverly D. would put her far in front of the field."

Our normal coterie of owners, friends, and associates went to Chicago with us. I had generated a lot of enthusiasm in the newsletter I had sent out a couple of weeks earlier.

"This is it," I had written. "This is the most significant race that we have ever been in. This is the heavyweight championship fight, the Super Bowl, the last game of the World Series. We may never be in a race that means this much to us. EVER. When they turn into the stretch in the Beverly D. Stakes, and Miss Josh sees the finish line, she will see something sitting right past the line. And it is hers for the taking. It is a statue of a horse, a very special horse named Eclipse who won all of his races. And this statue is given out in recognition of a championship season. And it is right there in front of us! I can almost touch it from here."

I'm certain I could have found stakes races in which Miss Josh never would have been seriously challenged. I'm sure I could have kept her unbeaten from the Fort Lauderdale until the end of the year. Instead, I had set a torturous path for her. I had intentionally placed her in challenging situations and she had come through perfectly.

Additionally, I believed that a horse desiring to be a champion should meet all comers. As Paulick had written, Miss Josh was running a "nationwide campaign," and that was true. Before the year was through, she would have run at six different racetracks in six different states. I wasn't about to duck anybody.

Arlington Park was prettier than I had expected, and the staff was extremely accommodating. Since it was the biggest weekend of the year for the track, they went all out. They invited many other track officials from around the country, and the day before the Beverly D. in the hospitality room at the hotel adjoining the track, I was introduced to Howard Battle, racing secretary at Keeneland in Lexington, Kentucky. When he heard we owned Miss Josh, he said something very interesting.

"If she continues doing what she's been doing, you may be getting the golden trophy at the end of the season," he said. I cocked my head in disbelief.

What he meant was that if Miss Josh could continue winning, she would be a serious candidate for Horse of the Year, with which comes a golden Eclipse Award. I could see that he might be right. She already had won four stakes races in a row. If she won the Beverly D., the All Along, and maybe one other, she surely would have had a very impressive campaign, one worthy of Horse of the Year.

The weather was beautiful for the race, a late summer day that hinted at the arrival of fall. Time crawled by, and about an hour before the race a track assistant came over to me to tell me what was going to happen.

"You and nine of the party will be escorted by someone wearing a green jacket to the paddock," the woman said. "We will hold the elevator for you, and you will follow her into the paddock. The other twenty-seven people will follow this person wearing a red jacket. We will hold the elevators for them and take them to a position outside the paddock."

I appreciated the organization. Then came the curious part.

"After the race," she said, "CBS-TV will want to speak to you, so we will take you down the elevator and into the infield for the interview."

"You must think we're going to win," I said.

"Oh, yes," she said matter-of-factly.

"Then just give me the $300,000 right now so I can stop worrying," I joked.

Finally, it was time to go to the paddock, and we all followed the red and green jackets to our appointed places. I saw plenty of people I knew there, including Duncan Taylor, who had sold us Highland Mills so long ago.

"If I had known she was going to be this good, I never would have sold her to you," he kidded me.

The paddock area was crowded. It had that unmistakable feel of a big race about to happen.

I saw Tyson Gilpin and his wife, Tenchia. He wished us the best of luck, something that he had done continually since we had started winning races. Tyson was a very gracious man, the epitome of real class, and after we started winning stakes races, he also would call to congratulate us.

"I'm proud of you," he always would say, which meant a lot to me.

Miss Josh looked terrific in the paddock. When they put her in a stall to saddle her, she went right into her routine, curling her left front leg and wiggling this way and that while Barclay's crew struggled to saddle her. The tension in the place rose by the minute.

Laffit came into the paddock, decked out in our silks. A couple of photographers stopped him and snapped his picture, and then he and Barclay conferred. Laffit was in Chicago for the weekend and was scheduled to ride Tight Spot the following day in the Arlington Million. Finally, Barclay threw him on Miss Josh, and they headed out. I looked at Fire the Groom as she went past; she looked ready. French-trained Colour Chart also caught my eye.

As Barclay was leaving the paddock, a CBS correspondent pulled him aside and interviewed him, which left me a little uneasy. All at once it felt like the pre-race scene with Highland Springs before the Breeders' Cup Mile, before which a *Miami Herald* photographer summoned my wife and son to pose with Highland Springs in the background. It just felt like too many extraneous things were happening before the most important race in our history. To this superstitious owner, we seemed to be asking for trouble.

In his well-rehearsed trainer-speak Barclay told the CBS interviewer, "She's come into this race as good or better than she did the others, so I think she'll run well today."

Before our group split up — the larger half was going to watch the race from the trustees' room — I told everyone to watch the timer. Many had never been to a race before, and I wanted to give them a little insight.

"Watch that timer, and if you see them run a half-mile in forty-eight seconds or so, and we're not too far off the lead, we're in good shape," I explained. Then, as an afterthought, as something that surely couldn't happen, I mentioned, "If, however, they run that half-mile in forty-six seconds or less, and we're near the front, we're in trouble."

We made our way to the box, where we found Tyson and his wife sitting in a box next to us, watching Miss Josh and the other horses in the post parade.

"She looks good, George," Tyson said, and she did. She broke off from the post parade and galloped easily to the backstretch. She seemed less nervous than I was.

The Beverly D. is started on the final turn, giving the horses a decent run into the stretch the first time, and with a field of only seven, traffic wouldn't be a concern. Still, you never knew. They started loading the fillies and mares into the gate, and I snapped up my binoculars and focused on the stall that held Joshie. The field loaded quickly. This bunch of racehorses was professional, and it showed.

When the gate popped open, Joshie came out running. She was right on the two leaders from the beginning, and when she passed the finish line and went into the first turn, I looked at the timer. It said the horses had run the first quarter-mile in :21 3/5. I blinked, not comprehending what that meant at first. My gut reaction was that the timer had to be wrong. They couldn't have run so fast, not going that distance. Sprinters don't run that fast when they're going three-quarters of a mile. I focused my binoculars back to the field and saw Joshie was eager and Laffit was struggling to get her to settle back off the quick pace.

When they had run a half-mile, I looked at the tote board and saw the timer stop on :45 4/5. With Miss Josh near the lead, I knew this race was over. She was going to lose. I put down my binoculars.

All the planning, all the preparations, all the traveling … they all came to an end that afternoon in the first half-mile in the Beverly D. Miss Josh had overcome bad ankles, bad racing trips, and bad flights to get to the place where she could become a champion, but at the worst possible moment, she couldn't overcome her nature. She was a sprinter at heart, and she couldn't have picked a worse day to revert to type.

She actually ran a very good race. After those fast fractions, she took the lead between calls in the stretch but had no punch left when first Fire the Groom and then Colour Chart came to her. She was third, beaten four and a quarter lengths. As they pulled up, I felt my dream of making her a champion was over. Tyson could see it in my face when he turned to me. He didn't say anything. He just put his arm around my shoulder.

We tried to regroup and salvage the Eclipse Award campaign, and we needed a race in September to get back on track. There were two possibilities on the same day — the Violet Handicap at The Meadowlands or the River Cities Budweiser Breeders' Cup at Louisiana Downs in Shreveport, Louisiana, both grade III races on the turf. It wasn't a hard choice. We had won the Violet the year before, so I thought we wouldn't get much credit with the Eclipse voters by winning it again, and there was a huge disparity in the purses. The Violet carried a $75,000 purse; the race in Louisiana was $175,000. Barclay and I disagreed. He wanted to stay in the East, and I wanted to travel to the mid-South. We settled it in the paddock at Pimlico five days before the race.

We all were there to see Highland Crystal make her second start — and first one on the grass. While we were waiting for her to appear from the barn, I broached the subject with Barclay.

"I'd prefer to run Miss Josh in Louisiana," I said quietly.

He objected, saying she was a bit off in one foot, and he didn't want to ship her that far unless she was 100 percent. The problem was we would have to fly her to Louisiana in two days, while we could wait until the last minute to ship her to New Jersey. It was a valid point, but I still wanted to go to Louisiana.

Watching from outside the paddock, my mother could see what was going on, but she couldn't hear what we were saying. Then she saw something that convinced her of the outcome.

"When I saw George fold his arms and back into the corner, I knew we were going to Louisiana," she said. "I knew that Barclay could not change his mind."

Miss Josh had a wonderful flight to Louisiana. Even Barclay was impressed at how she reacted.

"I tell you, you could cut legs off this mare and put her on a plane, and she'd grow new ones before she landed," he said.

Going into the paddock, we were confronted by a happy-go-lucky Barclay. He was so relaxed he didn't even have his binoculars.

"How's Miss Josh?" I asked.

"She's perfect!" he responded breezily.

Mom, Sis, and I looked at each other.

"Barc's been kidnapped," I said, "and they've found a look alike to take his place."

The race itself was a carbon copy of her other wins. She sat off the early pace — the leader hit the half in :47 3/5 — before powering to an easy win in the mile and a sixteenth event. When it was all over, she had given every other mare in the race either five or seven pounds and a whipping. She set a stakes record of 1:41 2/5, the announcement of which set off a unique celebration by my mother.

"She set a stakes record!" she hollered in the winner's circle, leaping off the ground. "She set a stakes record!"

Rather than being elated that she had won, I was relieved she hadn't lost. She still had a chance at the Eclipse, I thought. But we had to keep on going down that road. And, oh, yeah … she won $111,240 that afternoon, the largest payday in her career.

We stayed over another day and had a blast at Louisiana Downs. Track officials gave us the skybox, and there was an open bar, hors d'oeuvres, a betting machine, a big-screen TV, and a balcony high above the finish line. It was great. We spent the afternoon watching the races and getting to know the occupants of the skybox next to us. It was rap star MC Hammer's family, who owned Lite Light, the top filly who was taking on the colts in the $1-million Super Derby the next day. Hammer wasn't there at that point — I think he came in that evening — but Mom didn't let that stop her. She got his father's autograph. I never did figure that one out.

We returned Miss Josh to Maryland and aimed her for her next race, the grade II All Along at Laurel Park. Three days before the race we were at the Laurel Turf Festival breakfast, where they drew the post positions for the races. Miss Josh had drawn the far outside, and when Damon Thayer, who was in the press office at Laurel at the time, came around asking questions, he asked if I was concerned at her being so far outside in a thirteen-horse field. Since there was a good run into the first turn, I really wasn't, and I quoted a famous jockey.

"As Angel Cordero said, 'If you're going to win it, you're going to win it from anywhere.' "

Thayer asked me about Miss Josh, and I told him that of all the races we had run in that year, the All Along was the one we most wanted to win. He queried me once more as to how our mare was doing.

"Well, she's really doing well," I said. "In fact, I think that if someone's going to win it, they're going to have to run the race of their lives."

Next to me, my sister cringed. I sat down. In my nervousness I had omitted one thing: the rest of the sentence. I had meant to continue with "… because I think she's ready to run the race of her life."

Without the concluding phrase, the sentence came off as bragging, even taunting, and that wasn't what I had meant to imply. I simply thought Miss Josh was ready to run the race of her life.

From there forward, everything fell apart for Miss Josh. It started to rain almost as soon as we left the breakfast, and it rained for the next couple of days. Then when Barclay worked Miss Josh two days before the race in the rain on the soggy turf course, she came back with a torn suspensory ligament right behind her left knee. There was no way that she could run in the All Along, and the vet said her recovery would take a considerable amount of time.

We went to the dinners and parties surrounding the Turf Festival, keeping quiet our bad news. The night before the All Along, Joe DeFrancis, president of Laurel and Pimlico, made a little speech congratulating the winners of the races on Saturday, and ending with, "And all of Maryland is pulling for Miss Josh tomorrow in her quest to win the Eclipse Award." I felt my heart sink into my stomach. Of all the races I wanted to win, the All Along was at the top of the list. We had almost won it the year before when she was just starting to get good, and now Joshie was a recognized stakes horse. As a racing fan, I really wanted to win the biggest turf race for fillies and mares at our home track. Now we weren't even going to run. I felt terrible. The next morning we scratched her and though downcast we remained hopeful we would get another chance.

We tried to bring Miss Josh back to the races, but after months of rehabilitation, she tore the same ligament again when she was put back into serious training, so we retired her.

She had won five of her last six stakes races, and with a bit of good racing luck she could easily have won seven stakes in a row. She had campaigned honorably across this nation and never ducked a challenge. And when she was asked, she left everything on the track.

In November, Miss Alleged won her first race of the year, after five starts in France and one in this country, when she upset the grade I Breeders' Cup Turf. A month later she won the grade I Hollywood Turf Cup, beating colts both times. She won the Eclipse Award for turf mares. Miss Josh was third in the voting. We weren't invited to the Eclipse Awards banquet.

Chapter 28

While Miss Josh was campaigning for an Eclipse, her half sister, Highland Crystal, had started her racing career. Second in her first two starts, she broke through with her first win, going a mile and a sixteenth on the dirt on September 27. Then she wheeled right back on October 8, and in her first allowance race on the grass she won by four easy lengths, the most impressive performance of any horse we had ever had at that point in their careers. Uncharacteristically, Barclay was very high on her from the beginning.

"This is the best horse you've ever bred," he said after the allowance win.

I scoffed. "What about Miss Josh?" I asked. "She's going to win a million dollars and an Eclipse Award."

"Highland Crystal will win three million dollars and five Eclipse Awards," he countered.

Of course, I hoped he was right, but, frankly, I didn't see it. Miss Josh had a classic look and a champion's heart. Highland Crystal was a little thing, long in the back and Roman-nosed. She was nowhere near as attractive as Joshie, but I had to give Crystal her due. She had done more than Miss Josh or Highland Springs had at the same age, and they went on to become multiple graded stakes winners.

After a couple of wins, we jammed Highland Crystal in the last graded stakes race for three-year-old fillies in Maryland. Inexperienced though she was, she actually ran very well. She took the lead from the start and held on well most of the way around before finishing fifth, beaten less than two lengths. That race was on Breeders' Cup Day, and we watched the Cup races on TV while waiting for her race. When longshot Miss

Alleged won the Breeders' Cup Turf, my mother was very pleased.

"I like it when fillies beat the boys," she said.

That race, of course, was the main reason Miss Alleged won the Eclipse Award. Be careful what you wish for …

Highland Crystal finished the year by winning an allowance race at Aqueduct in New York, taking her earnings to almost $49,000 for the year, the highest first-year earnings for any horse we'd ever had.

We went to Florida with Highland Crystal and Royal Mountain Inn for the 1992 winter racing season. Rita, Michael, and I spent that winter in Hallandale, one mile from the beach and one mile from Gulfstream Park. I would frequently bring Michael Barclay, who was two, with me in the morning and we would hang out at the barn. One day jockey Julie Krone came by to talk with Barclay, and she met Michael. She crouched down to talk to him. He showed her his chest-length scar from his open-heart surgery, and she showed him the scar on her arm from her latest riding accident. When we went home, I said, "Michael, tell your mom who you saw today." He thought mightily before saying, "A jockey."

"That's right, but which one?" I asked. He thought and thought before saying, "The little one."

Even though we were having a lot of fun in Florida, our racing luck wasn't so good. Highland Crystal was third, second, fifth, and finally first in allowance races at Gulfstream. Julie rode her in a couple of them and won with her in March. I had thought we would see our filly progress over the winter, but she seemed to have hit a plateau. My aim was to win every time we ran, and I really didn't care for a horse that didn't have a great desire to finish first. I was beginning to think I didn't understand Highland Crystal at all.

Royal Mountain Inn made his first start on April 11 at Calder Racecourse, about ten minutes inland from Gulfstream. The big gray gelding was fifth, beaten more than six lengths, running three-quarters of a mile on the dirt. It was about what I expected. Three weeks later at Pimlico he ran third in the same kind of race, again beaten more than six lengths. Kent Desormeaux rode him that day, and when he jumped off, he said he didn't think much of his effort.

Finally, on Memorial Day 1992, we got him on the grass in a mile maiden race at Belmont Park. We had never asked a maiden to take on the tough horses on the New York circuit, and while I was eager to see him run on the turf, I wasn't so sure he matched up too well with the usual bunch of classy horses in New York.

Royal Mountain Inn had been named for the restaurant owned by my in-laws. My father-in-law, Helmut Hemmerich, had fought for the German army in World War II, had been shipped to a Soviet prisoner of war camp after the conflict, and after returning home — weighing ninety pounds — had decided that America was the place for him and his young bride. Not speaking English, the couple settled on Long Island, where they worked as domestics on a big estate. One day on a hunting trip to upstate New York, my future father-in-law — called Dutch by his American friends — found a saloon/restaurant in Johnstown that was for sale. When he got back to Long Island, he asked his wife, "Inge, do you think we could run a restaurant?" "Sure, how hard could it be?" she replied. "I can cook, and you can tend bar; how hard could it be?" They soon learned.

They started out serving three meals a day, seven days a week, and gradually cut back, discovering, as do most people who run restaurants, that there is more profit in serving dinner and drinks than by serving lunch, or especially, breakfast. By the time I got to know them, they were working Friday and Saturday nights and Sunday brunch in a place that seated about forty people. They sent two kids through college, bought a farm, lived the American immigrant story. They got a big kick out of our horses. I'd make a tape of our winning races and send it to them, and whenever we'd visit the restaurant, they'd pop the tapes in, and everybody in the restaurant would get to see our horses win over and over again. That was okay with the patrons, as, for the most part, everybody in the place had probably bet on them. Many people came up and told me what they had done with their winnings, which included paying for lovely vacations to exotic places.

When we went into the paddock for the Belmont race, I felt certain Royal Mountain Inn would be 5-1 or so in the odds. When the odds changed for the first time, he was listed at 7-5. I stared at the tote board.

"How can that be?" I asked, incredulous. Then I answered my own question: "It's Johnstown money. Everybody up there must be betting on him."

I was right. When Rita's brother went into the off-track betting parlor in Johnstown that day, the teller at the betting machine knew why he was there.

"I know … you're betting on Royal Mountain Inn," the teller said. "Everybody's betting on Royal Mountain Inn."

Mike Smith was the rider, and he hustled Royal Mountain Inn out of the gate for the mile contest. After a quarter in a quick :22 3/5, our boy was third, barely two lengths back. He stayed right with the leaders until they hit the stretch, and when Smith asked him to run, he lengthened his stride. Watching him come to the leader, it seemed that every other horse in the field was taking three strides to our two. Up in Johnstown, the OTB was packed with people who had bet on him. I was later told that when he took the lead, the place erupted in cheers. They could see there was going to be extra money in their pockets that night. Royal Mountain Inn opened three lengths by the eighth pole and track announcer Tom Durkin said he was "sharp in victory" when he won by four and a quarter lengths. I looked at the timer. He had run a mile in 1:34 flat, really good time, and he had done it easily. It seemed we had another good horse in the barn.

Flying home that afternoon, I could barely contain myself. Royal Mountain Inn had run an extraordinary race, and he had done it without pressure from the rider. By that point I had been around two stakes winners, had run a horse in the Breeders' Cup, and had sent one to California to win a grade I stakes. Royal Mountain Inn had just won the most impressive first race on the grass of any horse we ever had owned. My mind was whirling, and it concentrated on one object: the Breeders' Cup. If he could run a mile in 1:34 in his first time on the turf, he certainly was a better individual than Highland Springs or Miss Josh, and to me that meant that we should aim him for the Breeders' Cup Mile at Gulfstream Park in October. I had no doubt that by the time that rolled around, he would be good enough to win it. I was so excited that night I could barely sleep.

The next day brought a splash of cold reality. Barclay called to say Royal Mountain Inn had chipped his ankle and needed an operation. He was through for the year.

When we returned to Maryland with Highland Crystal that spring, after a so-so seventh in the Jenny Wiley Stakes at Keeneland in April, she ran third in the Lady Baltimore Handicap in May, giving Highland Mills her fourth stakes performer out of her first five foals. I received a note from Kentucky breeder Bill Landes, farm manager of Hermitage Farm in Goshen. I had met Landes years earlier, and I had found him wise, funny, and helpful. I called him from time to time to get his opinion about possible breeding choices for our mares.

"George," the note went, "if I have to read about another stakes winner, stakes-placed or near champion out of this mare, I'm going to be sick!! Seriously, congratulations. It is a mare like this that all of us smaller breeders are looking for. I'm happy for you and proud of you."

I appreciated the sentiment. It wasn't unusual. People who knew us knew how long it had taken us to get one horse that could win two races in its career. We had paid our dues. We owned one mare, and we competed head to head with billionaires. It was a good story.

We entered Highland Crystal in the June 14 Penn National Budweiser Breeders' Cup, the springboard for Miss Josh's career two years earlier. She lay just off a decent early pace in the mile and a sixteenth race, was sent to the lead on the turn under jockey Edgar Prado, and drew off to win easily, winning in faster time than Miss Josh had done two years earlier.

We nominated her to the Matchmaker Stakes and went back to

Atlantic City for the third straight year. When we arrived at the track, however, it was raining buckets. Track officials said they were going to run this race — the headliner for the meeting for turf mares — on the grass, no matter what. I was ready to run, but Barclay wasn't certain.

"If I had only one good horse (which was our situation at that point), I think I'd scratch her," he said.

We debated and finally decided to go. Edgar Prado was in to ride Highland Crystal again, and the rain stopped by the time they were in the gate. Highland Crystal came out of post position number six, and when they sprang the gate, the horse to her outside, the John Veitch-trained Plenty of Grace, inadvertently stepped on her foot. Highland Crystal, who had plenty of natural early speed, broke at the back of the pack and found herself sixth in the run through the stretch the first time. Thrown off her game to some extent, Highland Crystal needed a steadying influence. Prado held her together, calmed her down, and let her race in the middle of the field down the backstretch. She was about four lengths behind the leaders, but there were five horses to maneuver around when the field turned for home. Favored Radiant Ring got the first jump and took a three-length lead over Highland Crystal in the homestretch, when Prado finally got her outside horses. She kicked into high gear and flew down the stretch. I couldn't tell where she had finished when they hit the line, but the photo showed her second, only three-quarters of a length behind the winner, Radiant Ring. It was a very impressive performance, and watching it on video afterward, Barclay repeated what he had said earlier, "This is the best horse you've ever owned."

"If she were the best horse we'd ever owned, she'd have won the race," I responded. Yet even I, the skeptic, had to agree she had run a top race.

This was the point at which we went wrong with Highland Crystal. Two years earlier Miss Josh really hadn't been a factor in the grade II Matchmaker. We took her back to Maryland, won a $60,000 stakes race, and she went on and got better from there. Because Highland Crystal had run so well in the Matchmaker, we decided to raise the ante. We aimed her for the grade II Diana Handicap at Saratoga.

Looking back on it now, it's easy to see our enthusiasm, yet we really were looking only at her past two races. She had won the Penn National Budweiser Breeders' Cup and then had run a game second in the Matchmaker. Fair enough. But if we had gone back further, we would have seen that she had run third and seventh in her two previous stakes races. If I could do only one thing over in the horse business, it would be this: I would have stepped back and run Highland Crystal in a smaller stakes race in Maryland or somewhere nearby. She would have won and not had to give 100 percent, and I think she would have had a better career.

Yet we weren't thinking like that at the time. We went to Saratoga and ran her in the August 21 Diana Stakes. Edgar Prado handled Highland Crystal well, keeping her out of trouble all the way around in the mile and one-eighth test. She sat third, two lengths behind the leader all the way to the top of the stretch, and then Prado sent her after the leader, took a short lead in mid-stretch, and fought all the way to the wire. In the final one hundred yards, Ratings ran at her from the inside and then Plenty of Grace ran at her from the outside, and at the finish, it was a three-horse photo for the win. Highland Crystal was the ham in that sandwich, faring the worst in the bunch, beaten by two very short noses. Plenty of Grace — the one that had stepped on Highland Crystal's foot in the Matchmaker — took the win with Ratings second. My sister took the loss hard, weeping after the race, which was an unusual occurrence. Usually, she was pretty stoic about a loss and saved her tears for when we won but not that day.

It had been a terrific performance, and there was no question Highland Crystal had left everything she had on that Saratoga turf course. I came to regret what I had asked her to do at that time.

The day after the race, as Veitch drove into the Saratoga backstretch in his Jaguar, he spotted Barclay, a long-time friend. He pulled up next to where Barc was standing, put the window down, and held up the

Saratogian Pink Sheet (a section of the newspaper so called because it's actually printed on pink paper) that showed the photo finish, with Plenty of Grace's nose on the wire first. The photo showed that Highland Crystal was beaten about six inches for the victory. All this time, Veitch, who had trained the likes of Alydar, said nothing. Barc looked at that and emitted a phrase that would have made a sailor proud. Veitch drove off a small distance before stopping, leaning out the window, and saying, "Rude letter to follow?" Barc laughed.

We had decided to sell Miss Josh at the 1992 Keeneland November breeding stock sale because, quite simply, she was too valuable to keep. We simply could not afford to breed both her and her dam to high-priced stallions. We had won a couple of stallion seasons by finishing first and second in the Matchmaker, but neither stallion seemed to suit either Highland Mills or Miss Josh, so the seasons were used for a mare my sister had bought in 1987.

There was something else in the decision to sell: Miss Josh's success as a broodmare was not a sure thing. I have always believed that success in breeding and success in running are different. One requires genetic ability; the other, athletic ability. Highland Mills was useless as a runner, but she already had produced three stakes winners. She was proven. Additionally, I agonized about Miss Josh's feet, and every time I did, I came to the same conclusion: There was no guarantee her babies wouldn't get those feet. In a few words, she was too risky for a small outfit like ours. After we retired Joshie, we sent her to Hidaway Farm to wind down from racing and to get ready for her new life. She seemed to adapt well enough, hanging out with the other maiden mares and being readied for the sale. We saw her when we went to Kentucky for the fall yearling sales, and she looked a picture. Tom Hinkle did a terrific job with her, especially her feet. He had her shod with glue-on shoes, which were easier on her as they did not involve hammering nails into those thin-walled hooves.

Highland Crystal came back from the Diana Handicap and ran next in the grade III Violet Handicap at The Meadowlands. The race was odd in that there were no clear front runners, so when most of the horses came out of the gate, their riders took hold of them and tried not to take the lead, generally the antithesis of a race run in America. Finally, Highland Crystal ended up on the lead, and I had a bad feeling about that. Then, as I looked at the timer and then at her, I could see she was not rank and the time wasn't too fast. All around me, co-owners were worrying out loud about her position, yet I was thinking that it might be okay. I wasn't sure, of course, but I thought that since she was running easily and since the fractions weren't too fast, that she might be able to go the entire distance in front. She turned into the lane with a one-length lead. Inside the sixteenth pole Edgar Prado hit her left-handed, and she began to drift out to the right. Sitting right behind her was Irish Actress. A space opened along the rail, Irish Actress accelerated. We watched in concern as she cut Highland Crystal's lead to a half-length, a neck, and then a head. Finally, thankfully, they hit the wire, and Highland Crystal had held on.

With Highland Crystal's win, Highland Mills had produced three graded stakes winners from her first five foals, an extraordinary achievement. Yet, when I looked at the tape of the race, I wasn't impressed. The contrast between Highland Crystal's win and that of Miss Josh two years earlier couldn't have been starker. Miss Josh had exited the Violet Handicap with wind in her sails. She had finished strongly against a half-million-dollar runner. Highland Crystal had barely held on, and Irish Actress wasn't the only one making up ground on her. I didn't have a good feeling heading into the October 17 All Along.

In my pre-race analysis of the All Along, I thought that if Highland Crystal ran her normal race, the worst she would do would be to finish second. She didn't. She ran a bad last, beaten almost twenty-two lengths. Edgar Prado said afterward that she had bled "big time," but when the vet looked in her air passages, he saw no evidence of blood. That meant the bleeding — if that in fact was the problem — had to be much deeper. She wouldn't have run that poorly if she could have breathed properly. She was not lame and had no other apparent maladies, and since she never been a head case, we thought that Prado had to be right. It took awhile, but Prado's analysis eventually was proved correct.

A month later Miss Josh went through the sales ring. Tom Hinkle had several horsemen look at her to estimate her value. The range was $175,000 to $350,000, and I thought their estimates were low. I predicted she would bring $400,000 "plus one bid." I didn't know if that one bid would be $10,000 or $100,000, but that was my guess as we went to Kentucky. We set her reserve at $349,000.

When it was nearly time for her to be sold, I waited behind the sales arena as she came up from the barn. She entered the walking ring and got on the muscle, as if she were in the paddock before a race. She perked up her ears, scattered the other horses in there, and finally had the place to herself.

The bidding started at $25,000, very low for a mare like that, even for 1992, the low ebb in the Thoroughbred market. The market had been in decline for eight years, but still, I expected the bidding to start at $100,000; however, the auction got rolling, moving from $25,000 to $50,000 to $75,000, and then $100,000, in about ten seconds. It went to $200,000, then $300,000. There it began to run out of steam. I think it was down to two bidders, and we hadn't reached our reserve. It hit $325,000, and someone came right back at $350,000. Beside me, my sister said softly, "She's gone."

But the bid went to $375,000 and then $400,000, where it stalled. The auctioneer stopped the proceedings to say, "Remember, this mare was an Eclipse Award finalist last year for best turf mare in America."

Prodded thus, someone in the crowd offered a bid of $425,000, and then it was over. My sister was crying, and I was straining to see who had bought Miss Josh. When I saw Seth Hancock of Claiborne Farm sign the sales ticket for one of his clients, I was overjoyed.

"Claiborne bought her!" I told my sister, and we jumped up and ran out where we caught up with Hancock. I shook hands with him and thanked him for buying her. My sister shook hands with him as well, before dissolving into copious tears again. That seemed to take Seth aback.

"Now, you're welcome to come visit her any time you like," he said.

To me, it was the best of all worlds. She would be just a few miles from where she would have been had we kept her ourselves. In addition, she was at Claiborne, a farm I respected greatly.

"She'll be going to some of the best stallions in America," I told my sister, "and we'll get to see her all the time. What could be better than that?"

With our big earner — Miss Josh — gone, we had to look around to find a horse, or two, that could carry the stable. We knew the money Joshie had earned for us would quickly go out the door, especially with our having paid $127,000 that fall for a stud season to Seattle Slew for Millsie. The late basketball coach Al McGuire used to say that to succeed in basketball, a team needed "an aircraft carrier." He meant a good big man. In racing, to succeed, one needed a good Big Horse. Who would it be?

We sent Royal Mountain Inn and Highland Crystal to winter in Florida for the 1993 season. Highland Crystal knocked around in a couple of races, finishing a solid third in the December 19 My Charmer Handicap at Calder, then turning right around and running a bad twelfth in the Joe Namath Handicap at Gulfstream at the end of January. But she didn't show any sign of bleeding in those efforts. Finally, after she was eased, beaten fifty-six lengths, in the grade III Suwannee River Handicap, the vet saw a massive amount of blood in her nasal passages. He gave her furosemide (known as Lasix), a diuretic that lowers the blood pressure in a horse and helps prevent bleeding. Barclay put Highland Crystal into a nice mile and a sixteenth overnight handicap, and instead of quitting in the stretch as she had been doing ever since the Violet Handicap, she accelerated strongly to win by a neck. She seemed to be back on her game.

We brought her back to Maryland and ran her in the grade III Gallorette Handicap, and she was a close fourth. Two weeks later we sent her to Monmouth Park, and she was fourth in another stakes. And two weeks after that we sent her back to Penn National for the race she had won the year before; she was fifth, beaten by four and a half lengths.

The close-but-no-cigar finishes were frustrating. We were sure that the Lasix was working, but she just couldn't seem to get over the hump. Or maybe she simply was running into better horses. Or, maybe something else was at work. The day after the Penn National race, Barclay called.

"Highland Crystal has a fracture of her hind leg," he said. "She needs an operation to put some screws in it."

We sent her to the surgeon in Maryland, and as far as we were concerned, she was through as a racehorse. After all, she was five years old, and while she was pretty sound, we were going to lose eight months or so of training. By then she would be six, and there wasn't a lot of upside in running a horse that age.

Royal Mountain Inn, the big horse — literally — had returned to the races in March, finishing fifth and third in allowance company at Gulfstream Park. He then found his way back to the winner's circle after taking an allowance race at Hialeah Park on April 10.

The race was extremely rough. Royal Mountain Inn was checked hard at the first turn when a couple of horses came over on him, and he dropped back to eleventh in the twelve-horse field. Watching the tape of the race later, I noticed he couldn't be seen until the top of the lane. Ninth on the turn for home, he accelerated, split horses, and won easily. The announcer called out, "This would be an amazing performance!" as our big gray waltzed to the lead.

A little more than a month later the Mountain, as we called him, returned to Belmont for an allowance race at a mile and a sixteenth. Julie Krone rode him for the first time, and he "walked his beat," as one reporter wrote afterward. *The Blood-Horse* magazine, covering the grade III Saranac Stakes at Belmont, noted the winner of that race had not been the fastest turf runner of the day and that Royal Mountain Inn "looked like a future stakes winner blitzing the field." He won that allowance race in a time of 1:40 flat, after a mile in 1:33 4/5. The Saranac, a mile race, was run in 1:34 1/5.

In full flight, he looked impressive. A massive gelding whose coat was getting whiter by the day, he stood out in any field, and when he kicked into high gear, his mane and tail — white with streaks of dark gray and black — extended beautifully.

Following a mantra of ours — "We want to run our horses against the worst horses we can find for the most money we can find" — we sent Royal Mountain Inn back a month later in a mile allowance race. New York racing rules being what they were, we couldn't run under the name of Bonner Farm, as we did in every other racing state because that name was already taken. We needed a new stable name for that one location, and my sister and I came up with Steadfast Stable, as we thought that we had been steadfast in sticking with our dream even when we couldn't win a race to save ourselves.

Going around the big turns at Belmont Park — the largest racetrack in North America at a mile and a half around — seemed to suit the Mountain. As large as he was and with as long a stride as he had, he was at a disadvantage when asked to go around the smaller turf courses like the one at Gulfstream Park. In this allowance race, just a one-turn event at Belmont, Julie Krone had him close to the pace, and then when she asked him for run, he exploded past the leader in the flick of a tail. He was a length back, and, then, whoosh, he was three in front and pulling away. He won by six easy lengths and hit the timer in 1:33 2/5, a second off the course record. Steven Crist, writing for *The Blood-Horse*, put a brief note at the end of his article that week:

"Royal Mountain Inn followed up his smashing May 15 allowance victory with another on June 12. The four year-old half brother to Miss Josh is ready for stakes company."

I wrote to Crist to thank him for the kind words, and he responded with a lovely note.

"I have long admired your horses, and especially Royal Mountain Inn," Crist wrote. "Beyond the fact that he has consistently earned very high ratings in the time figures I compute, I have been struck since his maiden victory by his unusually swift acceleration. He has that intangible look of a really good one."

We had never won a stakes race at Belmont Park, yet Royal Mountain

Inn was favored in the grade II Red Smith Handicap at a mile and a quarter on the grass. When a horse named Carterista flew away from the gate and opened eight lengths on the field, while setting ho-hum fractions, I looked at the timer, looked at the leader, and looked at the Mountain. Jockey Julie Krone didn't seem concerned. All the way down the backstretch, she left the Mountain alone while he raced five-wide. With about a half-mile to go, she asked him to pick it up. He responded immediately, cutting into the lead. As he closed with two others on the turn, I doubted for the first time whether he would win on the grass. The three of them were moving as a team, and he was outside, having to travel farthest. But my concern lasted only a couple of seconds. He came roaring off the turn, blew past Carterista, took the lead, and opened up, crossing the finish line three lengths ahead of Spectacular Tide and Share the Glory, one of Paul Mellon's horses. The Mountain ran the last half-mile in under forty-seven seconds, really impressive at that distance.

The headline in *The Blood-Horse* of July 24, 1993, read, "Make Room for Inn," and reporter Bill Finley, after saying that post-July 4, pre-Saratoga racing at Belmont is some of the dreariest racing in the New York racing calendar, then wrote:

"This is not an exciting time. All of which makes it so unusual to see an exciting horse."

Finley recounted Royal Mountain Inn's career to that point and stated, "The storyline was going something like this: beating up on weak company … might be a top-class horse … must prove more. The new storyline is much simpler. This is a very good horse."

Royal Mountain Inn also impressed Julie Krone.

"He has the presence of a good horse. He's calm and intelligent and even though he finishes with his ears up, I think he does that because he's bored. He's better when he's near horses, but he explodes so fast that no one can stay with him," she told Finley.

Highland Mills' produce record now read: seven foals of racing age, seven starters, seven winners, four graded stakes winners plus a stakes-placed horse. After the Red Smith I received a call from Kip Elser, a well-respected horse industry professional, congratulating me and asking me, basically, how I had done it.

"Well, I did have a reason for breeding to Vigors," I said, somewhat defensively.

"I'm sure you did," Elser said.

"There were some things in the pedigree cross that I liked, and, besides, I respected and liked Vigors," I responded.

It was true. The breeding of Highland Mills had not been a haphazard affair. Starting with Lucy's Axe, I had studied and studied Millsie's pedigree, going back more than one hundred years. I looked at every horse in that pedigree and what it had accomplished, and what I learned I applied when we bred Millsie. I may never understand anything else in life as well as I understood Highland Mills. When we selected a stallion for her, it was because we wanted to achieve something in particular. In breeding Highland Mills to Vigors, we were looking to add some stamina, and with Royal Mountain Inn's easy win at a mile and a quarter, it appeared we had achieved that.

I knew Royal Mountain Inn was the most talented individual we had ever campaigned. His victories came so easily, and in such good time, that the question became, "just how good is he?"

People like to anthropomorphize animals, horses in particular. Highland Springs was willing and kind. He gave what he had every time he ran, but sometimes he seemingly suffered from an inferiority complex. Miss Josh was pure competitor who left it all on the track. She always gave 100 percent, but she had her limitations and we needed to plot her races carefully. Highland Crystal seemed to win when she was the best horse in the race, but she didn't seem bothered if she lost.

With Royal Mountain Inn — well, I don't think we ever got to the bottom with him. I feared no turf horse on the planet when Royal Mountain Inn was running well. He had NFL star quarterback Michael Vick-like talent, and all I had to do was to pick his spots and keep out of his way.

Chapter 30

After winning the Red Smith, we had two paths we could take with Royal Mountain Inn. One went to Saratoga, where we had enjoyed so much good luck in the past. We could run in the mile and an eighth Bernard Baruch Handicap on August 11. The race carried a $100,000 purse and a grade II rating. Or we could go to Chicago and run against easier horses in the $250,000, grade II Arlington Handicap on August 8 at Arlington Park. The race was at a mile and a quarter, just like the Red Smith. It was an easy call.

Additionally, if the Mountain were to win the Arlington Handicap, he could wheel right back in three weeks in the million-dollar, grade I Arlington Million. The prep race would give us an idea of how he handled being shipped to the Midwest and whether he liked Arlington's turf course, so that's where I wanted to go.

Complicating the matter, however, was a virus making the rounds at Arlington. If we went to Chicago and the horse caught the virus, he might be out of action when the big grade I turf races were being run in the fall. We debated the issue and finally decided to stay and run at Saratoga. The decision didn't feel right at the time, and it felt worse when I arrived at the track the day of the race.

The Bernard Baruch was to be run on the seven-furlong inner turf course at Saratoga, and that was a problem for the Mountain. His stakes-winning half siblings all had handled tight turns with aplomb, but he was a different horse entirely. He had a long stride and found the bigger courses much more to his liking. I hadn't thought too much about which of the two turf courses would be used at Saratoga before we entered the Baruch, but when I saw it on race day, my first thought was, "It's just like

Gulfstream Park," where the Mountain had never won. I didn't think he would appreciate the tight turns, and I was right. I truly wished we had gone to Arlington Park for the Arlington Handicap and its larger course and longer distance.

The Mountain stayed close to the leaders all the way around, but he couldn't accelerate on either turn. He lost by a length to winner Furiously, who ran the distance in a sparkling 1:45 2/5, and by a nose to the favorite, Star of Cozzene.

A couple of days later Barclay called to say Royal Mountain Inn had bone chips in both front ankles. Though my heart sank at the news, I retained some optimism. The Mountain had come back to run well after the first operation on his ankle, so I was hopeful he would do the same after the second. Still, with the big money turf races in the fall — the Man o' War, the Turf Classic, and the Breeders' Cup Turf — staring us in the face, having him on the shelf was very discouraging.

The problem with Royal Mountain Inn was part genes and part physique. Highland Mills hadn't been too sound when we bought her. She tended to throw horses with talent but with soundness problems. Highland Springs had chipped a knee, but it was the wear and tear on his ankles that eventually forced him into retirement. Miss Josh had ankle chips that never seemed to bother her and poor feet that did. Highland Crystal seemed to be the soundest of the bunch on a day-to-day basis, and she had fractured her hind leg. Now Royal Mountain Inn came along, a huge horse who ran very fast on turf courses that tended to be concrete-like in the summer.

When the surgeon got into the ankles — especially the one being operated on the second time — he saw significant damage. Barclay told me later the surgeon said it looked like "a bag of marbles" and he had cleaned up as much as he could but he was not optimistic.

"I don't think he'll ever run again," the surgeon had told Barclay.

Of course, we rejected that prognosis. Our horses had always been able to come back from surgery, we thought, and this one will do it again. Still, we had to make plans based on that gloomy prospect. All at once we had no runners. Broadford, the three-year-old Spectacular Bid gelding out of Millsie, didn't have much ability. He won a little claiming race at Delaware Park and was claimed from us for $8,500. For us to make a go of it in the horse business, it was imperative we have income from racing. We needed some help, and that made us take another look at Highland Crystal. We had intended to sell her as a broodmare prospect, but now the situation was different. I called Barclay and broached the idea with him.

"Could she come back?" I asked.

"I think so," he said. "The fracture was very clean, and it was an easy operation to fit the pieces back together."

We decided to try to bring her back, but we needed money immediately to carry the business forward. I came up with a plan. We re-syndicated Highland Crystal, selling half of her to new investors for $100,000, with the first $100,000 from her expected sale the following year at the Keeneland November auction going to those investors. We planned on this being a one-year deal, and our aim was to earn some money and to increase her value as a broodmare prospect. We raised the cash in about a week.

When Highland Crystal returned to the races in March 1994, we were not encouraged by her first couple of trips. She finished fifth in two starts in Florida allowance races, and when Barclay returned north, we entered her in an allowance race on the evening of May 7 at Garden State Park in New Jersey. The race was supposed to be on the turf, but heavy rain that day caused it to be taken off the grass. Only my brother-in-law and I went to the race, and after we checked into our hotel, my sister phoned, saying Barclay had been calling her and urging her to scratch Highland Crystal. I couldn't see why. We had scratched her a time or two before when a race had come off the grass, but she had won on the dirt before, so I wanted her to run. Maybe she could handle the slop; maybe she couldn't. The only way to find out was to send her out there and let her go. Besides, she had about six months left in her racing career, and I couldn't see how running her could hurt.

When we got to the track, I went to the racing secretary's office to renew my New Jersey license. Sitting there, filling out forms, I could overhear a man in the office on the phone, maybe with the racing secretary.

"Yes, the man from Bonner Farm is here right now," he was saying. "I'll ask him." He turned to me.

"You do know that the race has come off the grass, don't you?"

"Uh-huh," I replied.

"The man said, 'Uh-huh,' " he told the caller. Then he listened before asking me another question.

"And you're still going to run Highland Crystal?"

"I think so," I said.

"The man said, 'I think so,' " he said.

Now I was nervous. I thought Barclay was trying to scratch the horse, and I really didn't want to argue the point. Knowing he wouldn't scratch her without my consent, I decided to hide until it was too late. My brother-in-law and I went into the grandstand and sat down until it was time for Highland Crystal to come to the paddock. We met Barclay and his assistant trainer there, and not a word was said about the track condition.

I actually relished the opportunity to run. If Highland Crystal could run anywhere near her capabilities, she should win. All she was facing were turf horses running on the slop, and that often is a recipe for an easy win if the horse can handle it. Soon after the field broke, Edgar Prado placed her right behind the leaders. Then with a half-mile to run, he made his move. When she opened up on the final turn, the announcer called out, "Prado takes a look around, but he hasn't even cut Highland Crystal loose yet!" She looked like she was jogging and the others were under a drive. Her lead increased.

"They're inside the eighth pole, but this race is loooonng over!" the announcer called.

She won by an easy five and a quarter lengths, and she looked like she hadn't done a bit of hard work.

Meanwhile, Royal Mountain Inn was progressing at Chanceland Farm in Maryland, where Highland Crystal had gone to recuperate before him. My sister and I went over about once a week to monitor his progress, and we were encouraged, as owners tend to be. After he recovered enough to get out of the stall, the Mountain spent time walking around the shed row. Then they put a rider on his back and started to give him some easy jogs. The ankles seemed to be holding. Throughout the winter of 1994, Royal Mountain Inn continued to progress, and by the time spring arrived in Maryland, he was on the track and moving as he always had, much to his surgeon's growing amazement.

"There's no way that horse should be able to walk," he said one day while the Mountain went past in a breeze. "No way."

In all fairness to the surgeon, he probably was right. Royal Mountain Inn's ankle problems should have stopped most horses. You can't go into an ankle and take out chips but so many times, and the Mountain had already had three operations, two on one ankle and one on the other. His terrific size and the speed at which he ran should have caused problems for most horses, but — as Sandra Forbush had said so many years earlier, when he was just a weanling — "He is so light on his feet, especially for a big horse." He was able to overcome what would have stopped most horses because, quite simply, he wasn't like most horses. To a certain extent, good horses make their own rules. Otherwise, it's difficult to understand how a horse like John Henry could have won grade I stakes races when he was nine. They're able to do it because they are special.

After her allowance victory, we rolled Highland Crystal right back into a grade III stakes at Garden State, and she was a good second to a horse owned by one of the sheikhs, beaten a half-length. Then she went back to Penn National for the third straight year for the Penn National Budweiser Breeders' Cup Handicap, and she was third, beaten one length with Prado aboard. Not bad, but not really good enough. At that point she had won about $30,000 since she had broken her leg. The new investors weren't going to make any money at that rate. I looked for another race, an easier race, and I thought I had found one. It was the River Downs Budweiser Breeders' Cup at River Downs in Cincinnati in mid-July. We had never run a horse at that track or even in Ohio. But the purse was $150,000 added, so if she won it, it certainly would be worth the van trip.

By summer Royal Mountain Inn was close to a start, and Barclay thought we might bring him back in a stakes at Laurel Park on July 4. The only problem was we didn't have a jockey. Julie Krone had a commitment that day, so we started looking elsewhere. I called Bob Meldahl, Laffit Pincay's agent, to see if the talented jockey could come, but he couldn't either. Chatting with Meldahl for the first time since Miss Josh ran her last race almost three years earlier, I mentioned we were aiming Highland Crystal for the stakes at River Downs and asked if Laffit would ride her. He agreed. Then I told Barclay, and he wasn't as keen.

"I told Prado he was going to ride her," he said. "Now you're going to have to call his agent and tell him he's not!"

It really wasn't anything against Edgar. He had always ridden well for us, but Highland Crystal was getting close but not winning. If Laffit hadn't been available, I would have stuck with Edgar. I wasn't really in the market for a new jockey, but Laffit … well, we had had some good luck with that canny rider, and I thought he might shake her up a bit.

Instead of the July 4 stakes, Royal Mountain Inn returned to the races in an allowance race at Belmont Park on July 9, with Julie Krone aboard. The big gelding showed absolutely no signs of rust or injury. He won in a walk, running a mile and a sixteenth in a sparkling 1:39 4/5, two-fifths of a second off the course record. His mile split was 1:33 3/5. The race carried a nice prize in addition to the purse money. We won a jeroboam of champagne, and we carried that monster-sized bottle on the plane home with us and then on to Kentucky for a pre-race party the night before the River Downs race.

We had only one little problem going into that race. The minimum weight Laffit could make was 117 pounds. Tracks allow five pounds of overweight, but no more, so it was imperative that River Downs have Highland Crystal carry at least 112 pounds. About two weeks before the race, I called the racing secretary's office to tell them what I needed. Highland Crystal had won one small allowance race in fifteen months. I feared they would weight her too lightly.

I got someone in the office on the phone and asked him how much weight Highland Crystal was scheduled to carry. He said something surprising and insulting.

"Oh, yes, Highland Crystal," he began. "I looked at her past performances … She doesn't look like much to me."

I couldn't believe that someone would be so rude. Luckily I had a response.

"Really? Well, she looks good enough to get Laffit Pincay to ride her in the race," I said. His mood changed immediately. Laffit, after all, was a Hall of Fame rider and a multiple Eclipse Award winner.

"Laffit's coming here?" he asked, disbelief in his voice. "He's never been here before."

That changed his tune. We talked about the weight, and she got 115, which was fine. I was ready to hang up, but he wasn't.

"Now Laffit, Laffit's coming here, right?" I told him he was, and we ended the conversation on that note.

The night before the race, my family — mother, father, wife, son, sister, brother-in-law — chilled that champagne and popped it open, and there was a general feeling of good will. I had studied the horses that were running, and I felt comfortable Highland Crystal could beat them, if she ran her race. Even my sister was confident, which was very unusual.

"We're going to win this race," she said.

The next morning my wife, Michael, and my parents and I got into our car in Lexington to make the hour and fifteen-minute ride to River Downs. With my sister and brother-in-law in another car, and with other people driving to the race with us, we had a bit of a convoy on the road to Cincinnati. All told, we numbered thirty or so.

"Well, let's go get the money," I said. In the backseat my mother was carrying less optimistic thoughts, she later told me.

" 'Get the money,' right," she had thought. "We're going to go up there, and it's hot, and she hasn't been running well, and he thinks we're going to 'Get the money.' My son has lost it."

River Downs turned out to be a delightful place. In spite of the guy's tactlessness when I called the racing secretary's office, everyone from the parking attendant to the tellers to the wait staff was pleasant. It was a terrific afternoon.

Laffit rode one race before the stakes race, to get ready, and won that, so he was batting a thousand going into our race. We met Barclay in the paddock as he brought Highland Crystal over.

"How's she doing?" I asked tentatively.

"She's perfect," he barked.

That definitely was a good sign. Barclay wasn't in the habit of saying that too often, but whenever he did, our horse always won.

Laffit came in, and I was close enough to hear Barclay's instructions to him before he put him up.

"It looks like the winners are coming from behind, so take a hold of her coming out of the gate and let her make one run from the back of the pack," Barc said.

We made our way outside to some box seats in the grandstand. These boxes were designed to hold six people, but I took one for myself. I wanted to have enough room to cheer, if the opportunity presented itself. I badly wanted her to win.

They opened the gates, and in a flash, Highland Crystal had taken the lead. It was the exact opposite of what Barclay had said, but the early pace was slow, and she was eager, and Laffit gradually got her to relax and sit just off a couple of horses. Freewheel, the favorite, sat a couple of lengths farther behind, under Pat Day.

On the turn the announcer called out, "Three furlongs to run, and the real running has started!"

Laffit moved Highland Crystal up to the leader, collared her, and all at once I knew we were going to win.

"There's not a horse on the planet that's going to pass her today," I thought, "not with the way she's running and with Laffit riding her." I started cheering madly, and — without realizing it — began moving across the aisle into another empty box.

The lead horse took Highland Crystal wide, and Pat Day cut the corner with Freewheel. Highland Crystal began to make up ground. I could see Laffit hadn't even turned over his stick as the horses pounded down the lane. That was heartening. Freewheel caught up to Highland Crystal inside the eighth pole. Laffit tapped Highland Crystal's flank a couple of times, and that was it. First by a half-length. In jubilation I picked up one of the plastic chairs in the box and brought it down sharply. It exploded into a thousand pieces. No one around me noticed. They were too busy celebrating the first stakes victory we'd enjoyed in exactly twelve months.

Our group trooped to the winner's circle, glad to be back in that hallowed place. My mother was so happy that she kissed Laffit right on the mouth, a shocking display for one brought up properly in the Deep South. When someone asked Laffit why he had come to River Downs, a place he had never been in his thirty years of riding, he was succinct and complimentary to us.

"I know when they call me, they've got something good."

Highland Crystal won $95,460 that afternoon, the biggest payday in her career. A reporter asked me why we had come to the race. I guess I seemed flip with my remark, but it was the truth.

"Because we thought she could win," I explained simply.

The track had a little party for us after the race, and I went around the room introducing myself to the people I didn't know. Finally, I found the man I had talked to on the phone a couple of weeks before. It seemed as if he was still unsure of what had happened and why.

"You know, me and the boys were sitting around, trying to figure out why Laffit Pincay would come here to ride that horse, and finally one of the reporters said, 'Well, he's not coming here to eat the chili.' You know Cincinnati's famous for chili?" he said to me. I didn't. He continued with the reporter's quote. "He must think he's got a good chance to win."

Chapter 31

*H*ighland Crystal's victory in Cincinnati proved to be her last. She closed her career with a seventh, a fourth, and a seventh in her final starts, all in stakes, and then sold for $260,000 in November. Still, she won $130,000 that year and increased her value about $100,000 or so. Not a bad achievement. Her new owner, William Reed of Mare Haven Farm, bred her to Storm Cat, A.P. Indy, and Storm Cat in succession, and the third foal sold for $1.35 million, so I'd say her owner did all right as well. None of her foals, however, have made much noise at the track.

That also has been the case with Miss Josh. Bred to Forty Niner and then Storm Cat, she was sold in foal to Lure for $500,000 to an English breeder at the 1995 Keeneland November sale. A year later she was sold at Tattersalls in England to Australian breeders Stratheden Stud in Tamworth. We got in touch with the farm and maintained regular contact, and in the summer of 2001, Rita, Michael, and I went to Australia specifically to see "our" mare. Judy Marvene, the farm manager of Stratheden, put us up for a couple of nights and let us see Joshie. It was a wonderful, late-winter afternoon in Tamworth when we went into the paddock to see her again for the first time in seven years. She looked great, and we think she remembered us. She sighed contentedly when we scratched her back and hung her head over Rita's shoulder. It was very touching.

Judy then took us on a tour of the stud farms in the area, and we went to five or six gorgeous outfits in a 450-mile round trip drive. Judy introduced us to the farm owners and managers as "the people who bred Miss Josh." The people knew who she was.

In August 1994, we shipped Royal Mountain Inn to Saratoga, and Barclay decided to run him in a handicap race at a mile and an eighth for a decent purse. But the race was being run over the tiny inner turf course again — the one upon which he had failed the year before in the Bernard Baruch. I didn't watch the handicap in person, but Royal Mountain Inn ran his usual race, attending the pace and running on in the stretch. He again showed he couldn't make up ground on those tight turns, and he ran second. I was very disappointed with Julie's ride in that race and tried to change riders. Julie called me a couple of days after the race, and we had a long talk, and, I think, a meeting of the minds. We aimed the Mountain for the grade I Man o' War Stakes at Belmont Park nearly four weeks later.

Not only was the Man o' War Stakes named for the horse some consider America's all-time greatest, but it also had been won by my favorite horse, Secretariat. In 1994 it was going to be run at a mile and three-eighths, the longest distance Royal Mountain Inn had ever run, and the purse was $400,000. I knew that with his ankles the Mountain would not have many races left in his career.

The Man o' War was part of what they were calling Super Saturday at Belmont. The day, which dawned hot and muggy, featured six grade I stakes races, with most of the winners aiming for the Breeders' Cup seven weeks later. We had our usual group of thirty or so. Rita, Michael, and I were staying with some of Rita's cousins, and we got to the track before the first race. The day dragged, and whenever I left the air-conditioned Director's Room, where my family had enjoyed lunch, the heat and humidity hit me in the face. Finally, as soon as the sixth race was run, we gathered our group and headed to the paddock to await the Man o' War field.

By that time I had relaxed. I felt confident Royal Mountain Inn would win if he ran his race, and there wasn't a horse in the field I feared, though most of them had earned a lot more than his $190,000. Fraise was in the field and was the program favorite. He had won the Breeders' Cup Turf two years earlier. I saw his owner, Madeleine Paulson, in the paddock. Her husband, Allen Paulson, started Gulfstream Air and was said to have five hundred horses in training.

Prince Khalid Abdullah of Saudi Arabia, who rarely attended races, was in the paddock to see his horse Run Softly saddled. The paddock began to fill as the horses came in. The Mountain looked his regal self. He always had a presence. The way he strode around, you could tell he knew he was something special.

About fifteen minutes before the start, Julie Krone appeared and came right over to me. After our air-clearing discussion, she looked to me for direction even though Barclay always dispensed the jockey instructions.

"I'll ride him however you want me to ride him," she said, unprompted. "If you want me to stand on my head, I'll do that."

It was the only time in my life I've been able to utter words attributed to Oakland Raiders owner Al Davis.

"Just win, baby," I said.

My sister went through her normal routine of planting a big red kiss on the end of the Mountain's nose. On the closed-circuit TV, track handicapper Harvey Pack was talking about the horses in the field. He mentioned our boy, calling him "Royal Mountain." Pack said all he had beaten this year were allowance horses and that he would be carrying sixteen pounds more than he did when he won the Red Smith the year before. As usual, I discounted the idea that weight meant anything to a horse of his size. And his win earlier that year at Belmont had been accomplished in excellent time. And one more thing: Barclay Tagg was a steeplechase rider, and jump jockeys tended to understand how to get a horse ready to win a distance race.

Saddled, the horses headed toward the track, and we made our way to our box seats. Royal Mountain Inn was in the outside post position in a nine-horse field. Thinking of whom we were going up against, I had to laugh.

There were Fraise, the Paulson horse, and Run Softly, Prince Khalid

Abdullah's horse. There were Solar Splendor, two-time winner of the race, and Fourstars Allstar, winner of the 1991 Irish Two Thousand Guineas and a full brother to Fourstardave, whom Highland Springs had beaten five years earlier. Turk Passer was rumored to be sitting on a big race, and Kiri's Clown had the speed to steal the race if he could set slow early fractions. And there was Flag Down, who had done most of his running in France. France's top jockey, Cash Asmussen, had come to town to ride that one. And of that bunch of distinguished horses and horse owners, we had the favorite.

Even though Royal Mountain Inn was coming into the grade I race off a loss in a much less difficult race, and even though other horses had won millions of dollars more than he had, the bettors saw something the program handicapper discounted: Royal Mountain Inn had never lost at Belmont Park. He was a perfect five for five, and most of his victories had been accomplished in an easy manner and in fast time.

I was calm as I watched him warm up. He was easy to see, being the only gray horse in the field. When he stepped onto the turf course, I could see his ears go up. He was ready. Up in the booth, Dave Johnson was talking about the field for ESPN. He went through each horse by post position and finally got to us.

"And Royal Mountain Inn, who's never been beaten on this turf course, is the favorite at this time at nine to five."

He didn't sound convinced. He and racing analyst Chris Lincoln talked about Fraise.

"Trainer Billy Mott said that he really hasn't gotten a course he's wanted; well, he has a firm turf course, just to his liking today," Johnson reported.

The first eight horses went into the gate like the pros they were. Royal Mountain Inn, though, started to rear up and banged the gate, just like he had done before the Red Smith.

"Settle down," track announcer Tom Durkin said into the microphone. "Royal Mountain Inn is acting up a bit in his outside post position."

They all broke well, with Kiri's Clown taking the lead in front of the longshot Palashall. Cash Asmussen angled Flag Down over to the hedge, an ideal position to save ground. Julie Krone allowed our boy to sit about two lengths off the lead. We were three wide going around the first turn. Jockey Mike Luzzi had Kiri's Clown on the lead and was doing his best to slow down the pace. Unlike with Miss Josh, the early pace was never a factor with Royal Mountain Inn. He had been able to win off just about any pace scenario before, so I wasn't worried how slowly Kiri's Clown went. The field covered the first half-mile in forty-eight seconds, slow for that hard turf course.

"Kiri's Clown on the lead; the favorite, Royal Mountain Inn, well in hand on the outside in third," Durkin called. "Fraise is on the inside."

Kiri's Clown ran the first three-quarters of a mile in 1:12 1/5, and that meant he had achieved his mission of setting a dawdling pace. Royal Mountain Inn was two lengths back, with Krone well in command. Five-eighths of a mile to go, and she hadn't asked him to do too much. The field ran as a tight pack. It seemed to be anybody's race. As the horses took the turn for home, I could see our boy was ready. Julie took a quick peek to her outside and saw no one coming. She let the reins out a notch.

"Royal Mountain Inn is now revving up on the outside."

Inside a quarter-mile the pace quickened. Julie looked left and saw Flag Down on the rail and then looked right and saw Fraise outside.

"Kiri's Clown holding the lead by half a length … "

Julie drew her stick with her left hand but didn't hit him.

"… Royal Mountain Inn poised on the outside. Flag Down in on the rail, Fraise is full out!"

It was time. Julie popped the Mountain once, twice, with her stick. He surged.

"They're at the eighth pole, Royal Mountain Inn has a head in front, Kiri's Clown is fighting on valiantly on the inside … Flag Down is closing.

"… Fifty yards to the line, Royal Mountain Inn … Flag Down …"

Cash Asmussen had Flag Down in full flight by then. He had taken him outside the tiring Kiri's Clown, and he began to close on our boy. Being the professional he was, Asmussen saved every inch of ground he could.

All around me Bonner Farm people leapt around, screaming for Royal Mountain Inn to keep going, but I knew from the way he was striding out that he wouldn't get caught. I had already put my binoculars down, content to watch the final yards unfold.

"… Royal Mountain Inn holds on, with a jubilant Julie Krone aboard!" He crossed the wire a half-length in front.

It was the same margin that Miss Josh had won by in the grade I Gamely, but he had accomplished his grade I victory so much more easily. He had gone three- and four-wide on both turns and still had plenty left to hold off Flag Down in the stretch. It was a dominating performance.

"Perfect ride there by Julie Krone," Durkin opined for the ESPN audience, and it was true. She had ridden him well. I had been wrong to try to replace her. "She really didn't ask Royal Mountain Inn for everything he had until the last furlong, and that's when it counted today," Durkin added.

As the horses returned to be unsaddled, we were making our way to the winner's circle, all thirty of us. I could see people I knew applauding our horse's effort as we went past. It was a thrilling moment. Upstairs, Chris Lincoln and Dave Johnson were speaking for ESPN and their voices boomed over the track's loudspeakers.

"Royal Mountain Inn, the unofficial winner, in a surprise here in the Man o' War," Lincoln said.

"What race was he watching?" I thought. Johnson was more observant.

"The New York bettors are certainly savvy. Royal Mountain Inn didn't start out the favorite, but he ended up that way and was first under the wire, now six for six on the turf at Belmont Park," he said.

Royal Mountain Inn was jogging slowly to the gap that led to the main track and to the winner's circle. He looked unperturbed. His ears and tail were up, as if he had plenty of energy left. He came back to the enclosure as if he hadn't done anything more stressful than take a morning walk. Photographers from the New York papers and the trade publications took picture after picture as Julie circled him around, waiting for the groom to put a shank on him and lead him in. Barclay placed my sister's left hand on Royal Mountain Inn's bridle, and she and the groom led him in to terrific applause from all of us.

ESPN was showing the replay of the race by then and noting he had set a stakes record of 2:11 3/5.

"Now the fractions, three-quarters in twelve flat, that's pretty slow 'cause this course is very, very hard," Durkin said. He followed the field on the screen, saving most of his comments for the final eighth of a mile.

"… The last furlong of this mile and three-eighths marathon was sprinted home in eleven and four-fifths seconds."

The winner's circle photos accomplished, we prepared to receive the trophy. We had to wait for Barclay as he and Julie were being interviewed by Dave Johnson. Johnson spoke to Julie first.

"Hey, Julie, what were you looking around for there in the stretch?"

"Well," she replied, "there were a lot of class horses in there and some really big closers, and I had some horse turning for home, and I was hoping I was the jockey with the most, and I ended up being, fortunately."

Julie told Johnson what it was like to ride Royal Mountain Inn.

"I feel invincible when I ride him."

Johnson then turned his attention to our trainer.

"Stakes record, even with a half in forty-eight … Barclay Tagg … stakes record?"

"That's very nice. It's exciting," Barclay said. "I thought when they had those early fractions, and he was running that strong, if he won, it might be a stakes record."

"What's next?" Johnson asked.

"We're planning on the Turf Classic, if they invite us."

"I think you'll be invited."

"I hope so."

Later, when I broke down the late fractions, Royal Mountain Inn's performance impressed me even more. Yes, he ran the last furlong in :11 4/5, but he ran the last five-eighths of a mile in :59 1/5, the last three-eighths in :35 3/5. It was a superb performance, and it put him over $433,000 in earnings. A win in the Turf Classic in three weeks would add another $300,000, and if we went to the Japan Cup in late November — a representative from the Japan Racing Association had invited us immediately after the race — a victory there would add a whopping $1.7 million more. He could go from having earned less than $200,000 in September to earning almost $2.5 million before December, and that could keep us in the business a long, long time.

Chapter 32

"Follow your bliss and don't be afraid, and doors will open for you where you wouldn't think there could be doors, and where there wouldn't be doors for somebody else."

Joseph Campbell, *The Power of Myth*

The day before the $500,000 Turf Classic, Barclay called to say Royal Mountain Inn was hurt and out of the race. It was his ankles again, and this time he couldn't come back. He had been the odds-on favorite for the race, which Tikkanen, who replaced him as the favorite, won. A few weeks later, Tikkanen also won the Breeders' Cup Turf, which we hadn't planned on running in, no matter what happened in the Turf Classic. The Breeders' Cup that year was at Churchill Downs, and the track's seven-furlong course, with three turns in the mile and a half Turf, wouldn't have suited him well. If we had gone anywhere for another race that year, it might have been the Japan Cup. Horsemen who had been there before told Barclay that the turns were even bigger than at Belmont.

We returned him to Foxhall Farm in Flint Hill, Virginia, where he had been as a weanling. Sandra Forbush put him into a paddock with Highland Springs, the horse who had blazed our way in the beginning. It was very heartening to see those two half brothers who had done so much for us reunited. One was unbeaten at Saratoga; the other, unbeaten at Belmont. Few can say they have had such horses.

However, Royal Mountain Inn's retirement was an indication of things to come. It seemed that Bonner Farm was about to run out of good horses and good luck. Rejoyced, Highland Mills' 1992 filly by Relaunch, proved to be only useful. She ended up a stakes-placed winner of $111,000. My sister kept her as a broodmare, but she died when her fifth foal, a Chester House filly, kicked her internally and ruptured her intestine.

Then there was the 1993 colt by Seattle Slew. I hadn't wanted to breed Highland Mills to Slew as I didn't think he suited our mare too well, and with his stud fee of $127,000, we'd better be right. In spite of my trepidations, the resulting colt was strong and strapping, a dark bay. We named him Mills, after his dam.

He blossomed at two, and one day in March 1995, I called Barclay's barn in New York. Barc had taken a string of his better horses up there, and he took Mills because, with that pedigree, he had every right to be a good one. I personally didn't have a feel for him. I'd never had a good two-year-old, and I didn't know what Mills should be doing and when he should be doing it. I didn't know what to expect. I had heard some nice things about the colt, but those people weren't Barclay and his crew, who were pretty direct in their evaluation. After the horse had had a couple of light breezes, I talked to the assistant trainer. The conversation went something like this:

"How's Mills?"

"He's fine."

"But how's he training?"

"He's doing well." I felt like I was getting nowhere. May as well come right out and ask the big question.

"Well … what do you think? Does he look like he might be a decent runner?" The assistant paused before answering with conviction.

"George, don't worry about this colt."

That was a good sign. I hung up the phone feeling that maybe I had been wrong, that maybe the ones who had wanted to breed Millsie to Slew in the first place had been the prescient ones. Looking toward the future, I sat down with the other members of the partnership group in Mills: my sister, brother-in-law, mother, and Harrison and Eleanor Jones, who had been in on many of the horses out of Highland Mills.

"Okay, if this horse wins his first start, somebody's going to call and offer us a million dollars for him," I explained. "What will you all say?"

"We're going to keep him," they said. I decided to up the ante, rhetorically.

"Okay, let's be optimistic. Let's say he wins a couple of races and the Hopeful Stakes at Saratoga and then he wins the Breeders' Cup Juvenile. He's the champion two-year-old. Someone's going to offer … ," I was fishing, "… ten million dollars. What do you say then?"

"We're going to keep him."

I didn't like the way this was going.

"Look, if he's any good, we're going to have to sell him at some point and syndicate him for stud duty." That was the truth. In fact, in January of that year, I had received a letter from a prominent Kentucky horseman asking to be considered for stallion manager for Mills if he turned out to be a stakes winner. If he became the fifth stakes winner out of Highland Mills, I knew the farms would be making very attractive offers to stand him at stud. Still, my reasoning didn't convince any of the other partners. They wanted to keep him, no matter what. Left unsaid at that time was the idea he might be a total washout. He just couldn't be, not with his pedigree, looks, and the reputation he was developing at the barn.

In May, with Mills about one workout from a race, I got a call from a Kentucky horseman.

"Would you sell half of Mills for a half-million dollars?" he asked.

That seemed like the compromise I'd been waiting for: No matter what, everybody would make money, and we'd still have half the horse. I proposed the deal to the other owners, and they shot it down quickly. A couple of days later, the colt's future took a decided turn for the worse.

The vet said Mills needed operations on both ankles. He recovered, and when he was ready to go to the races seven months later, veterinarians discovered he had a paralyzed vocal cord that needed to be tied back. More time lost. His stud value was zero at that point, so we had him gelded.

With him in and out of surgery in New York and Florida, and recuperating in various locations, I hadn't seen him in more than a year, and when I did, I could barely believe my eyes. At two, he had been a terrific-looking individual. When I saw him again, he had grown so long in the back he looked like two guys in a horse suit. And he ran like two guys in a horse suit. We finally got him to win an $8,500 maiden claimer at age four, and we ended up selling him for $5,000. Some horses never seem to get any luck but bad luck, and he was one of them. After all the surgeries and the training expenses, he represented a $250,000 loss to us, maybe more.

We bred Highland Mills to Pleasant Colony in 1994, and the resulting colt made my heart beat faster. He was strong, correct, with a large chest, maybe a bit plain in the head — taking after both his sire and his dam — and he had an attitude that said, "I am going to be something!" Looking at him when he was four months old, I was thinking, "This is the best horse we've ever bred. He's put together better than Royal Mountain Inn. We're going to win the Belmont Stakes or the Breeders' Cup Turf with him. Or both!" We decided to name him Gilpin, to honor Tyson Gilpin.

One morning in December, Tom Hinkle called me. Gilpin had broken a leg in a paddock accident at Hidaway and had to be put down. He was insured, of course, but for about a fifth of what he was worth on the market, but the loss to Bonner Farm extended far beyond monetary. He should have been our next good horse, maybe a stakes winner at three, four, and five. Maybe even a stud horse. He was the aircraft carrier that Al McGuire had talked about. Plenty of great breeding farms had been built around one horse, and that one horse generally was a stallion. That's what Gilpin might have been for us, and with Millsie getting up in years — she was sixteen that year — it was unlikely she would ever have one like him again. The disappointing career of the Seattle Slew colt was a terrific setback, but one that could be overcome if we came up with another good horse. The loss of Gilpin, however, meant that all at once no horses were in the pipeline. Millsie had foaled Mills, been barren one year, had Gilpin, and then had not gotten pregnant in 1995. If she got pregnant in 1996, it would be 1999 at least — likely 2000 — before that foal could help keep Bonner farm going. It seemed like the handwriting was on the wall.

I had been through a nearly devastating seven years before we started winning with our homebreds, and then we had won graded stakes for six straight years. It had been a roller-coaster ride, and I could see we had reached the top and were headed downward. I wasn't going to go through that again, but I had one last plan — a Hail Mary if there ever was one — which I proposed to my sister and mother in 1996. Highland Mills was in-foal to Danzig. I thought if we sold her, she would bring in the neighborhood of $700,000. The market for Thoroughbreds had strengthened considerably since hitting bottom four years earlier, and I thought if we sold her and paid the stud fee, we still would have $500,000 or so to buy other horses, a combination of yearlings and broodmares. My sister didn't want to sell the mare that had done so much for us, and I understood. We decided to have an amicable split and she bought me out of Millsie and Rejoyced.

***

So, what had I achieved, after seventeen years in the game? I had set out with a motto: "Dedicated to breeding and racing the Champion." I had set out to breed the next Secretariat, and I hadn't done that. Of course, deep down, I understood a horse like that comes along once in a lifetime. He was the definition of brilliance to me.

No, I hadn't bred the next Secretariat, but what I did do, however, was find the essence of my being. I was down. I was almost out. I should have quit, wanted to quit, but didn't quit. I found resilience at my core, and all sorts of good things happened to me. It was a wonderful journey. Then, years later when I read the quote by Joseph Campbell used at the beginning of the chapter, it all made sense. I had followed my bliss. I had done the thing that made me happy inside, and doors had opened for me.

Some may think that I just got lucky. Maybe so. You've got to have good luck to be in racing. But you don't buck the kind of odds we faced with just luck. It was luck that put Highland Mills into our hands. But I believe it was skill that assembled a great team that worked well together toward a common goal. When Millsie ran so abysmally as a racehorse, most breeders would have thrown her away, consigned her to the ash heap of breeding and racing. We couldn't. She was one of only three mares we had, and all of them were important to us.

So ours is a story of success against great odds. We were able to stay in a difficult business for seventeen years by paying attention to details and learning on the job. After buying six yearlings and having four go to the races and only one win for us, I can point to a statistic: Every horse we bred went to the races, and all except one won. Horses that we bred and I managed won 55 of 167 starts, 33 percent. In stakes races, we won seventeen of fifty starts, a 34 percent clip. I'm pretty proud of that record.

When I talk about the time we had, people can tell how much I loved all of it, and they often ask why I got out. There are several answers, but it all comes down to the fact that I did what I set out to do. I proved to myself that if I ever got my hands on a good horse, I'd know what to do with it.

Sometimes they ask me whether I could do it again, and I have to say I think I could. I know I can manage horses. Frankly, I can't stand to lose, and I always imagined that the horses we owned hated losing as much as I did. That's why — after learning on the job — my number one goal was to put them in races where they could win.

Yet would I want to get back in, knowing how hard it is? That's a tougher question. Now Michael has gotten very interested in racing, and he is very keen to see a Triple Crown winner. He has rooted very hard for all of the recent candidates — especially, of course, for Funny Cide, who was trained by Barclay Tagg — and when Smarty Jones lost the Belmont Stakes in 2004, he was very disappointed. He turned to me and said after the race, "Dad, I think that you and I are going to have to breed that Triple Crown winner."

Now there's something to aim for! So would I get back in? The answer is … maybe. People have approached me about getting me to syndicate and manage horses for them, and I've turned them down so far. The situation would have to be right, but I can say I do miss the game. There was nothing like the feeling I got when we were winning. With Miss Josh and Royal Mountain Inn, I think I felt like an Old West gunslinger coming into town. No matter how fast the local gun fighter was, I knew I could take him.

The impact of our horses went far beyond what I ever could have expected. In 1994 I asked Sid Fernando, the breeding editor for *Daily Racing Form*, whom he would breed to Highland Mills, and he opened the question to readers. They printed fifty-eight responses, from all the well-respected pedigree experts in the world, as well as from casual racing fans. I was astonished. I had trouble believing that all those people would take the time to think about our mare, look at her pedigree, think about stallions, and write letters to the *Form* expressing their opinions. These were people whose opinions I valued, professionals in the business, but more than horse people were involved. A teenaged boy from the Bronx wrote in, offering his opinion about Millsie and her possible mates. And the letters were read by thousands. When I stopped Seth Hancock in November at the Keeneland sale to ask if we could breed her to his first-year stallion Lure, he seemed taken aback.

"You mean your big mare?" he said. "After all those letters in the *Racing Form*, you want to breed to Lure? Well, you've got it."

(It turned out that by the time Millsie foaled in 1995, Lure was on his way to being declared infertile, and Hancock graciously told us we could breed to any stallion at Claiborne Farm. When we chose Mr. Prospector, he said, "Well, it's not a pedigree that jumps out at me, but if you get a filly, you'll be jumping up and down, and if you get a colt, everybody else will be jumping up and down." Regrettably, Millsie had only one chance to breed to that great stallion, and she failed to get pregnant. If she had, I might still be in the game.)

A few years later I was interviewing Ken Tomlinson, who had recently moved to our area of Virginia. Tomlinson had been the editor-in-chief of *Reader's Digest*, and when he retired he went into the horse business, something he said he had always wanted to do. We were talking horses, and all at once the light went on.

"Wait a minute, you're that guy, that guy that had that mare ... Highland Mills," he exclaimed.

I acknowledged I was.

"You know, we were in an executive editorial meeting, and we spent forty-five minutes talking about who we'd breed to your mare."

So time has passed, and we've moved on. My sister and brother-in-law stayed in the game, racing the last two foals out of Highland Mills and the foals out of some of her daughters. They haven't had the kind of success that I would have hoped for them, but as we all know in the horse business, your next good horse might be the unraced one you've got in the barn right now. My mother, now almost eighty-five and still working five days a week, keeps her interest in the horses with my sister and enjoys going to see the babies in the spring at Hidaway Farm.

Barclay Tagg, of course, has gone on to greater and well-deserved fame as trainer of Funny Cide, winner of the 2003 Kentucky Derby and Preakness Stakes. It goes to show you the vagaries of racing. In the spring of 2002, I called Barc and chatted with him, as we do once a month or so to this day. He complained that he didn't have any good horses and that he was ready to retire, but that his stock market portfolio was down so much he didn't think he could. Little did he know that there was an unraced two-year-old gelding down his shed row that was going to take him places he had only dreamed about. Racing ... you just never know.

Highland Mills had two more foals for my sister and then was pensioned. She lived out her remaining days at Hidaway Farm before being put down in 2004 from laminitis. She's buried there. A small headstone tells the simple data about her life. It would take something the size of the Ten Commandments to share what she meant to all of us.

Highland Springs spent his last days at Foxhall Farm, dying from a paddock accident when he was sixteen. Royal Mountain Inn is still there, his coat a pure white, and we get to see him when we visit Sandra Forbush. Sandra, after a tragic car accident in which she broke her back in three places, has become an accomplished painter who paints portraits of horses, dogs, and the people that love them.

Miss Josh is still in production as a broodmare at Stratheden Stud in Tamworth, Australia. Her owner and I e-mail each other every couple of weeks, and the owner has promised to read Joshie some of the pertinent passages of this book. She hasn't produced a stakes winner, yet, but her first daughter, Nicole's Niner, produced a group III stakes winner in Singapore.

I'm the business editor for the *Fauquier Times-Democrat*, an astonishing thing for me to contemplate, since I never studied journalism. I got my job because someone at the paper had read one of my Bonner Farm newsletters, and when the former racing columnist quit, they asked me if I would do it, and I agreed. The paper may be one of few in America to have a horse sports editor, and the staff includes a polo player, a foxhunter, and me, a racehorse guy.

Our family still lives in Orlean, Virginia, in the middle of Virginia horse country. One of the local fox hunts often goes down our road when out hunting. Michael has taken to writing a column of his own for the paper — titled "Ready For Prime Time" — and he received his first media credentials to cover the 2005 Pimlico Special. He may well be the only fifteen-year-old in the world who subscribes to and reads *Foreign Affairs*, *Armchair General*, *The New Yorker*, and *The Blood-Horse*.

Why write this book? The idea came to me in a way while we were doing so well. Standing in the paddock before a stakes race, I often found myself thinking, "I wish this were happening to someone I know because I'd like to write a book about it." Frankly, because I was so close to the story, I thought I couldn't do it justice. I'm not sure I have.

I've now written stories about approximately seven hundred business people since I became business editor, and after a while, I noticed something curious. Most of these people were opening up new businesses, and for many the business represented the dream of their life, and they were scared. So I found myself telling my story to them — of how it was so bad for so long, and then of how it turned around and was so wonderful —

and I could see the story resonated with them, in spite of the fact that none of them were in the horse business. Finally, one day, one of them said something to me:

"You need to write a book," he said. "Kids need to know that they can have a dream and have it come true."

So that's what I hope I've done. Secretariat gave me the dream, which, while not impossible — for this is America, after all — seemed highly improbable. And then it came true. Thinking back on it now, I often get tears in my eyes over what our horses did. Truthfully, not a day goes by that I don't think of those wonderful horses and how they enriched our lives, and I know that I have been truly blessed.

Acknowledgments

When I re-read this book in its entirety, I discovered to my dismay I had not fully credited my sister, Bonner Young, and her husband, Tom, for the success of Bonner Farm. I regret that, for without them, there would have been no Bonner Farm, and thus no book. I also want to thank my parents. When I came up with the wacky idea of buying racehorses, they brought out the checkbook and wrote me a check.

I also was fortunate enough to have a wide-ranging group of people who played important parts in our success. One who ranks very high is the late Tyson Gilpin, who always supported our efforts and celebrated our victories. I miss him a lot. Next would be Sandra Forbush, whose excellent horse sense and steady encouragement carried me through some very rough patches. The partners we had over the years also contributed. Tom Hinkle of Hidaway Farm was a constant fount of common sense. Even when we hadn't won a single race, Seth Hancock of Claiborne Farm was always willing to help us with good advice. Duncan Taylor sold us Highland Mills, but that was just the beginning of what he did for us. Peter Pegg and Amy Adkins always helped us when we were looking for stallions for our mares. Bob Meldahl, agent for my favorite jockey, Laffit Pincay Jr., was a total professional. And as a racing fan, it was a tremendous thrill to me to have Laffit Pincay ride our good horses. I thank the staff of the *Fauquier Times-Democrat* who encouraged me to finish this book while working full time.

And finally, trainer Barclay Tagg, who brought us success. I truly believe Highland Springs and Miss Josh would never have become graded stakes winners without him. I am so pleased Barclay finally got the opportunity to show what he could do with a Triple Crown kind of horse in Funny Cide. I had seen that talent and focus a long time ago and knew that if Barclay ever got his hands on a horse like that, he'd know what to do with him.

Author

George Rowand was born and grew up in Richmond, Virginia. After attending Virginia Tech, where he received a degree in history, and the University of Memphis Law School, he began practicing law in Manassas, Virginia.

His life took a radical turn when he saw Secretariat win the Preakness Stakes, and on that day he decided he had to find a way to breed and own Thoroughbreds. In 1980 he started syndicating racehorses under the name of Bonner Farm, and after six dreadful years the horses had won one race. However, when the yearling fillies he bought were bred, the entire enterprise took off. He campaigned graded stakes winners for six consecutive years and left the business in 1998.

He now is the business editor of the *Fauquier Times-Democrat* in Warrenton, Virginia, and lives in the village of Orlean with Rita, his wife of 21 years, and their son Michael, 15.